LIVE. LOVE. LAUGH.
AND
MATES. MENOPAUSE. MISCHIEF.

My Fears And Tears Throughout The Years

STEPHANIE M. HOUGHTON

authorHOUSE®

AuthorHouse™ UK
1663 Liberty Drive
Bloomington, IN 47403 USA
www.authorhouse.co.uk
Phone: UK TFN: 0800 0148641 (Toll Free inside the UK)
       UK Local: (02) 0369 56322 (+44 20 3695 6322 from outside the UK)

Published by AuthorHouse 11/23/2022

ISBN: 978-1-7283-7516-8 (sc)
ISBN: 978-1-7283-7515-1 (e)

Print information available on the last page.

CONTENTS

PART ONE
LIVE. LOVE. LAUGH.

PART TWO
MATES. MENOPAUSE. MISCHIEF.

ACKNOWLEDGEMENTS
PART ONE

To My Dad
You were the best man I ever knew. I wish you were here. "Who loves ya baby?"

To The Houghtons & The Lemins & Everyone In-between
Never have I felt so whole, since finding you. At last, I belong. My family, my blood. I love you all very much.

To SJF
Thank you for this and for your acknowledgement of my genius. Takes one, to know one.

To My Friends
You are, and always have been my family since I moved to London, at the age of 22. I have been on the most incredible journey so far. For all the versions of me who have emerged over these fifty plus years, may I continue to evolve, grow, learn, inspired, and be inspired. With your support and love, I cannot fail.

Thank you, from the bottom of my heart.

Hello you!

For just over half of a Century I've now been on this planet. How on earth I actually made it thus far, frankly, is a miracle.

All these adventures are personal. Everyone's experiences are different, although some may be very similar; but it's how you choose to deal with them, which defines you.

Someone once said to me. "It's not WHAT you go through, it's HOW you get through it." How right they were.

I think the most important thing I learned along the way, is that people will do what THEY want to do, generally, and one can't stop that. One can only choose how one reacts to their decisions.

But always hold on to yourself. For you, my friends and family, hold in your hands all the magic in life that is required.

Thank goodness I paid attention in school in between the bullying and the bullshit, long enough to learn how to write, articulate and express myself in this magnificent medium of diction, grammar, words and humour. It's not always grammatically correct and I do have a propensity to swear (rather a lot). But it's me; bold and beautifully imperfect.

Live large. **Love** yourself.
Laugh at everything.
xoxo

PART ONE

LIVE. LOVE. LAUGH.

1 TO YOU, THE PLAYERS OF MY GAME

This is not a board game... but you're all pieces in MY puzzle.

Can't play Poker if the Aces are missing.

So don't think I'm dismissing any one of you.

There have been Snakes and Ladders along the way.

And this Operation is full scale.

But let me give you a Clue-do.

There's no sinking this Battleship – oh no.

You're ALL the key players in MY game.

No matter how big or small, the part you've played.

Has in some part, made me who I am today.

And some of you have kept me sane.

When I've lost the plot or been in pain.

So I just want to say.

Thank you. Thank you.

To each and every one of you.

'Because you ALL make up "My Crew".

And I'd be nothing (or much less for sure) without you.

As for the rules, well... you all know how bad I am at that.

RTFM – no Chance Card or Risk of that in this little Mouse Trap.

And I can hear some of you shouting "Snap"!

It may have taken me a while for this smile to feel real.

But now I'm finally seeing

That I'm a pretty awesome human being.

Trust me, it's taken a few fresh hands,

A good shuffle and some clever dealing, to believe it;

To say it out loud and really, REALLY mean it.

That you're all on my team, means I'm winning.

So thank you for playing along, while I found me.

I've won this round... now it's your deal.

24 October 2017

2 LU LU'S COMING

She ain't no ball-breaker.

She's a record breaker and a head shaker.

Watch her gyrate and move her body to the funky house groove.

She's a hip grinder and her moves are smooth.

She's the real deal, baby.

She's peanut butter; a bit of a nutter.

A number crunching, wordsmith thesaurus.

Listen to her lyrics as they drip with cockney rhyming slang.

But baby watch out for that smile, 'cause she bites with fangs.

She's a country girl at heart, like a sweet strawberry tart.

She'll keep you on your toes baby, and for sure You're gonna keep wanting more.

With flaming hair, she's the Queen of Hearts, like Lady Di;

She's the sum of her parts.

Take that and Lu Lu WILL relight your fire.

But don't play with matches baby, you WILL get burnt.

She'll punish you and teach you until you've learnt.

She'll drive you mad through the streets with her top off.

But baby you can't cop-off.

You have to work hard to get in HER car.

She's a fast track, no backpack wielding, and high-rolling entrepreneur.

With curves like Jessica Rabbit, she's got a Selfridges habit.

She's got a taste for fast cars and first class.

LV wraps her neck and Bella Poc bubbles fill her glass.

Keep out of her business or she'll dismiss you.

She'll take you higher; from The King's Road, back to Notting Hill.

And when she's done with you baby, you're gonna need a headache pill.

You'll get dizzy if you're not ready for this.

She IS Narcotic Venus.

She'll spin you right round baby, like a record baby.

But if you play it right, she'll treat you niiiiice.

You'll be the cat that got the Custard Creams.

She's fruity like Rhubarb, and sharp as a knife.

But she won't Crumble.

So get ready to Rrrrrumble.

When she gives you the go-ahead baby, take it steady.

But are you ready?

'Cause baby her favorite brew is dark and golden.

(Now rich and a little bit older).

So take a pew, 'cause there's a "Q" and when she's ready she'll tell you.

She'll take a shot and she shoots to kill.

Licensed to thrill and "try not to break it 007".

She's on a mission, and there's no better position than to be in her sights.

For your eyes only, baby.

Take the blindfold off and see what's what.

Do you really think you can handle that?

We'll see, 'cause this girl is Juicy.

So baby, you'd better hold on.

'Cause Lu Lu's coming, and the game is ON!

31 August 2014

3 LIFE - NO-ONE SAID IT WAS EASY

LIFE – no one said it was easy.
And if it were, would you value it more?
Would you love it?
Would you try to get better, be better?
Want more, have more, do more?

LIFE... it's hard sometimes, for sure.
LIFE is what you make it.
So make it big, make it loud.
LIVE it massive and tall.
LIVE it up and stand up proud.

Be good. Be amazing. Be silly.
Fill your days with
All the goodness you can touch and see.
Be EVERYTHING you want to be.

Try something new and give it a go
LIVE and LOVE and LAUGH every day.
LIFE - you better strap yourself in and commit.
Coz it's gonna get rough and you might feel a
bit sick.

It may throw you overboard. No, it WILL throw you overboard.
Sorry, more than once.
But you will stand up again and dust yourself off.
Because Life's for the taking, no doubt about it.

Your choice to LIVE. Your choice to LOVE.
Grab LIFE by the balls – this offer will expire.
It's not a rehearsal, this IS the main event.
So make it a SPECTACULAR showstopper.
Of everything you dreamed of being and doing and having or seeing.

LIFE - No-one said it was easy.
But it doesn't have to be dull.

28 May 2014

4 THE GIRL INSIDE THE WOMAN

There's a woman in my life, a girl that no-one sees.
It's not the woman in the mirror, surely that's just me.
She's distant and aggressive yet she reaches out for love.
But when it's given tenderly, she'll reject and rise above.

She wears my clothes and looks like me.
Although she sports a frown.
She'll not allow herself to dream.
Her nightmares bring her down.
This woman disbelieves that to have love, she is deserving.
And will retreat with caution, whilst she's quietly observing.

Her self-esteem goes up and down, self-worth a non-event.
How can I tell this woman that each moment should be spent.
Affirming and believing that the girl inside is true.
And the woman on the outside
Should embrace and love her too?

The woman on the outside knows that there's a missing part.
The girl who hides her pain deep down.
Needs peace inside her heart.
I'm trying to help the girl inside to accept the woman here.
To dispel my pain and agony, my wretchedness and fear.

It's a task that I must face with fortitude and nerve.
I must help her understand that yes, she does deserve.
I'll fight for love and unity and as one we'll kill the fears.
I'll do this for myself, for her and to cease the endless tears.

6 November 1997

5 DAMN YOU SAMBUCA!

Damn you Sambuca!
With your aniseed twist,
With one quick flick of the wrist
You're in me.

You're mine, but it is you who possesses me.
Caressing me, warming my chest, creeping,
seeping into my very being.
You seduce my vocal chords, as I hear myself
getting louder.
My language getting fowler and I'm turning into
a bloke,
As I choke on your power.

Damn you Sambuca!
With your aniseed twist.
With one quick flick of the wrist
I swig down another.
The flush of my cheeks get rosey.
And we all get a little more cozy, even rude.
As we collude in our union.

I'm dancing now, prancing waving my arms around.
To no apparent sound.
Think I'm the star, but I'm not.
I'm just a piss-head in a bar.

Damn you Sambuca!
With your aniseed twist.
With one quick flick of the wrist
With your aniseed twist.
Now I'm completely pissed.
Oh no... I'm gonna be sick!

8 April 2014

6 GOING TO THE GYM

Going to the gym used to be easy.
I'd finish an eight-hour day and training was breezy.
I'd cram down a banana or a protein shake.
And run to the tube so I wouldn't be late.

Protein shake blenders and creatine benders.
I'd pump iron for hours, like a half-back defender.
But that was when I was younger of course.
Now I'm more like a knackered old horse.

I set my alarm and have the best of intentions.
But there's always a more important distraction.
I'll stay in bed a bit longer, ("well I needed the sleep") I'd mumble.
But not able to justify, as my excuse is rumbled.

"To stay healthy and fit you must train 3 times a week"
Says the skinny instructor as she flexes and squeaks.
I went to the gym to work out yesterday.
But I couldn't be bothered, so I just ran away.

Well that's exercise surely, running from the gym.
I jest... There's no excuse really, for not doing my best.
I look okay (I justify) but when I'm on that beach next week.
I'll probably cry – "WHY OH WHY didn't I go to the gym?
This bikini doesn't exactly make me look slim.

So I finish this rhyme with a cursory nod.
To my gym bag, my shorts and my super sports bra.
Without which, I'm assured, I wouldn't get very far.
And remember that I'm lucky to have all my limbs.
So tomorrow – tomorrow, I WILL go to the gym.

2 April 2014

7 DETOXING

We seem to go through life being tempted and teased.
By everything under the sun that is mean.
To our system and shouldn't be eaten or consumed.
It's bad for our body, sugar, drugs, caffeine and booze.

So after a while, our bodies give up.
And we have to take action. Enough is enough!
So we invest in a juicer to get ourselves sorted.
And that big weekend out with our mates is now thwarted.

The major conglomerates push us to the max.
We now have to read every label and pack.
To ensure we're not ingesting a new kind of toxin.
That's the problem when we begin our detoxing.

It becomes an obsession. We must beat depression.
Must eat the right measures and take the right action.

Go to the gym, get a person trainer.
Have our nutritionist on a monthly retainer.

Yoga, Pilates, body pump and spinning.
Just so long as we're healthy, we know that we're "winning"!
Push away the old habits of Fish and Chip Friday.
Do a colonic spa retreat for your next annual holiday.

Spirulina, flaxseed, Omegas 3, 6 and 9.
Cut out the dairy and definitely no wine!
Spinach and broccoli and ginger and kale.
All go into the blender for the internal "de-scale".

Grapefruits and lemons, fennel and beetroot.
All manner of organics to make you feel good.
"But be careful you don't over-do it", they say.
"You could send your body off course, the wrong way".

So here's my advice, go gently when you start
to detox.
Because you could send your liver into toxic
shock.
"What?" I here you say. "That's a huge revelation!"
Now pass me the wine;
Well... everything in moderation.

11 May 2014

8 LIFE LESSONS

You can't put an old head on young shoulders.
But when you see the troubles of the world
Smolder in a young and beautiful soul.
The only goal is to ease the burden.
Even when no words can heal them.
Experience will enlighten and then,
Slowly, as they grow, they
See more clearly.
Or at least, we hope so.
So we stand by and watch them wrangle.
Looking for the better angle;
But never finding it, so they struggle on.
Life is shit sometimes.
While some look like they have it easy.
Don't be fooled by it or reeled-in by the Facebook profile smiles,
The snippy Twitter tweets and the Insta-heart-art of sunsets and twilight kisses.
It's nearly always a farce.
A gallery of ideal perception,
Is actually a snapshot of deception.
'Cause you'll never know the cards they're dealing with.

Darkest tasks from their past that make their mark and break your heart when you see it breaking theirs.
But they're helpless and defenseless.
Whilst your older and wiser amour from years of experience deters it.
And they can't wear it,
Till they've earned it.
That's life.
And it can hit hard sometimes.
Platitudes like "what doesn't kill you makes you stronger"
"The grass is always greener"
"If I knew then what I know now"
"Half empty or half full" glasses of bullshit solutions
For short-cutters, lazy fuckers and fakers;
The takers of this world, not the givers.
But will I give up?
Not a chance.
I'll never change the fundamentals
Of my stance.
Having learned to quiet my demons, at least for the time being,
I still respect their ability to create an instability within me.

But I will fight until my dying breath to deflect and reject them.

Stay on my trajectory.

The only way is up and it's ok to look down to remember.

But don't waiver in the darkness of your past.

'Cause misery loves a friend and I don't intend to feed it.

So keep moving and share your wealth of knowledge.

Help your friends with every struggle.

Even when it's such a muddle.

Just be there. Showing that you care.

Try to help repair.

But remember...

You can't put an old head on young shoulders.

And when you see the troubles of the world smolder

In a young and beautiful soul.

The only goal is to ease the burden.

Even when no words can heal them.

More's the pity.

'Cause life can be gritty sometimes.
And whilst these life lessons
Don't lessen the pain,
At least you gain a resistance, in some part.
To stop your heart breaking again and again.
Well, that's the plan.
So hold on and teach.
Hold your arms out to reach someone.
Knowing that you'll never save everyone.
But at least you tried.
Through the years of experienced tears you've
cried.

Life lessons are hard. It's true.
But older is wiser, is stronger
And younger isn't always better.
High-insight doesn't really exist.
So the life lesson is this...

You can't put an old head on young shoulders.
Sometimes it's just better to be older. And that's
it!

30 Sep 2017

9 THANK YOU LIPPED INK

I'd like to say thank you to Lipped Ink.
More specifically, Sarah and Mark (Mr T).
For giving me the chance to express myself
Quite literally. In word. At Open Mic Night.
These nights, when strangers trust enough
To share their talent and lay themselves bare.
How they dare to give with such eloquence and
grace.
And know that this is their time. Their space.
To do what they were born to do.
A medium loved by many, but actually tended
to, by so few.
With love, we feed each other's souls.
And watch every seedling as it grows.
I'm just a baby here and you can probably see
my fear.
The nerves which eat me up before I stand
before you.
Shaking, with my poem book in hand.
Ready to read, ready to share.
And to bare my soul. To express the experiences
I would normally hide from other prying eyes.
But to speak to you about such things, seems
easier.
You can keep your therapy sessions, all terribly
formal.

Or just talk to your friends to help you feel normal, but here.
In this place. Where I feel safe, comfortable and inspired.
With you all encouraging me, pushing me – no training required.
No exams to take here, nor levels to reach.
Just be yourself, be honest and true.
Just start with "Hello!" and "How do you do?"
"I'm Stevie, and erm, I'm new!"
You're not here to tread on toes, or show-off.
There's no competition here. Just rhyming rendition.
"But it doesn't always have to rhyme." Someone said…
Next time then, maybe I tell you a story instead?
So here I stand, with gratitude in heart and hand.
To say thank you to Lipped Ink.
More specifically Sarah and Mark, (Mr T)
For giving me the chance to express myself.
Quite literally. With you. Right now. Right here.

2013

10 I'M ANGRY

I'm angry.
And I know I'm not the only person.
Watching the news, with a terse-looking frown on.
I see politicians lie and people die in
forest-fires and tower blocks.
Bombing in the Eastern blocks and terrorist cells
rising like the pox.
Spreading hate and venom in the name of Allah.
200,000 people dying of Cholera, in Yemen.
In two thousand and seventeen?
A disease, the likes of which we haven't seen
in hundreds of years of history.

Things are bad. The world is damaged.
People's decency is being ravaged.
Like the rain forests of the Amazon;
Once an abounding cacophony of purest healing
herbs and plantation.
Is being stripped bare of its natural habitation.

But EVERY nation it seems, is failing our planet.
Human egos rising and spewing utter nonsense.
Their agendas becoming the lynchpin of our ruin.
Spin and Chinese whispers, gleaning conspiracy
theories.
Dealing hands to conquer and divide us.

Bad-mannered and dis-enfranchised teenagers
Running riot on the streets, stabbing and looting.
CCTV everywhere, but never on, when you need it.
Gunshots ringing in our streets, now a sound becoming normal.
It's tragic, and we're all losing our ability to believe in magic.

I'm angry.
And I know I'm not the only one.
Who stares in disbelief at what's REALLY going on?

Sitting in my living room, watching politically driven news feeds.
Lying about death tolls to protect the "leaders" of our communities, who are only given "P45" immunity for the actions of their cost-cutting, blood-sucking, self-serving reasons.
Officials who WE voted for, in a "bureaucratic civilised society"?
Don't make me laugh.
It's comedic, like a French farce.

Where's the truth?
We need to find it.
Even Trump, the "Leader" of the Free World's
an idiot!
De-stabilising people's faith in politicians.
While celebrities are posting selfies and "tweeting".
It's a free country, but we're bleeding to death,
slowly, but surely.

Nowhere for the people to run to.
No help for the people who have none.
Communities scramble to look after their own.
(While Simon Cowell makes another song
To line his pockets and raise his profile again).
Round and round like sheep we follow.
Being fed their lies and still, we swallow.

Yes, I'm angry.
But hey, I'm one of the lucky ones.
I've got a flat, a car and a job.
Even got a couple of pets.
But as I rush to help my peeps in trouble.
My tears won't help, so my anger doubles.

If I could save the world, I would.
But I can't. I'm just one person.
Do you think that's how Messrs. King or Mandella felt?
(Not that I'm anywhere near their heavyweight belt status.)
It's a hiatus. And we're all losing patience.

But if we ALL pulled together, we might.
Stand up TOGETHER and fight, for what's right.
Make having an ego illegal.
Hold our heads up and be regal.
Teach people how to be humble again.
Show ALL religions that women ARE equal to men.
That it's ok for a man to love a man.
And that it's perfectly wonderful to be a lesbian.
Welcoming the LGBTQ community and every degree in between
'cause everyone is different.
And shouldn't that be a reason to celebrate, not spread hate?
Children who are taught LOVE, will give it.

Somehow respect and forgiveness isn't in THIS remit.
It's bullshit.
Holding hands across nations
and getting to know our neighbours.
Should be a given.

I'm angry.
And I know I'm not the only person feeling it.
But I won't be spreading it freely.
Because HOPE is at the end of my rainbow.
And everyone is welcome in my world.
Isn't that how it should be?

Prejudice and racism revolts me.
Diversity and differences ignite me and drive me.
Humans can be AMAZING.
But some of them need naming and shaming.
I'm afraid the human race is failing.
It's utterly heartbreaking.

So, if we're all here for a reason.
Why not make it count?
No more fighting, hating and stealing.
But replace these
With love, forgiveness, hope and PEACE.
Please.

Dedicated to the Grenfell Community.
14 June 2017

11 SOMETIMES

I sit and wonder sometimes
How you'd give your child away.
To someone else, a stranger
Just because 'he' wouldn't stay.

I often wonder sometimes
If she's thinking of me too.
And does she realise I know
What she must have gone through.

It makes me wonder sometimes
As I'm gazing into space.
Is it my reflection in the glass
Or could it be her face?

I'm sure she wonders sometimes
Just the same as me.
But does she feel the same such thing
Or just plain sympathy?

I'm sure that she remembers
And she feels from time to time.
That when she's sitting wondering -
I am too, sometimes.

4 March 1992

12 LOST AND FOUND

How apt I find myself aboard a train and write these words.
The Lost and Found department here's, the biggest in the world!

I'm on my way to see a person, very dear to me.
A woman who I met just once, then said farewell to me.
She held me in her arms so tight, was hard for her to leave.
But fate had different things in store for us and so she grieved.

I sit aboard this train today, to look into her eyes.
She was young and he had gone, this decision must be wise.
The woman who gave birth to me, but had to let me go.
She passed her child to someone else, to love and watch her grow.

As the train moves out, apprehension, excitement, fear.
But nothing crushes courage when your vision is so clear.
I will show her I'm okay; I'm healthy, fit and strong.
To prove to her that fate was right and that she did no wrong.

I'm comforted by words from friends, as they smile and wave goodbye.
I can see their admiration, and the love shine through their eyes.
These friends and lovely people, give me strength to live and love.
To face my life with fortitude, so I will rise above.

I'm on the train, I'm on my way, with butterflies in tum.
I'm on my way, I'm on the train...
I am going to meet my Mum.

8 May 2010

13 ALONE SHE STANDS

Alone she stands and waits.
Heart full of hope and nervous.
Train pulls in, she scans and darts.
Is she here? So anxious.

Shock of red alights with smile.
Big expecting eyes which search.
Is that her, I'm just not sure?
Is she here, (stomach lurch)!

Finally catch sight of each.
Both in equal awe.
Desperate to find, out they reach.
Together now, once more.

A Mother hugs her daughter tight.
Now a woman fully grown.
Forty years it's been a fight.
For the women they've not known.

A daughter reassures her Mum.
They will catch up now.
No more reason to be glum.
They'll teach each other how.

Similar in many ways.
But apart for such a time.
No more lonely, empty days.
Just happiness; sublime.

Complete, together; whole at last.
Their love will now sustain.
Knowing Mum and Daughter's love
Will not be lost again.

9 May 2010

14 MY REAL FAMILY

March this year has been a month of discovery.
Of learning and growing and love washing over
me.
You see I found my Mum and my brothers just
recently.
And I went home to Wales, to see my real family.

I sunk into their arms and their smiles as they
welcomed me.
And I honestly felt like I belonged somewhere,
finally.
I had a mum growing up, but I don't think she
liked me.
But that's a whole other story, believe me.

So, I went "home" to Wales, to see my real family.
They all hugged me tight and told me they loved
me.
I can't really express how it felt, what it meant
to me.
To go home to Wales, to see my real family.

I got drunk with my brothers and we all laughed, excitedly.

Went off to the pub saying "Mum, don't worry, we'll be home for tea".

As I watched the boys tease with an easy camaraderie.

I smiled inside, because now... they were part of ME.

At the table we told stories of past times and histories.

Of memories they'd shared, which I'd missed, unfortunately.

But we'll make some new memories now, I guarantee.

Because I'm finally home, and I'm with my real family.

2 April 2014

15 MY DAD

There's only one man in my heart.
And one who'll always stay.
I know that even when he's gone.
He'll never go away.

There's only one man in my heart.
Whose love will always be.
Truly, madly, deeply.
And will always comfort me.

There's only one man in my heart.
Who'll give me strength when I am sad.
There's only one man in my heart.
That special man's my Dad.

3 February 1996

My darling Dad passed away two weeks after I wrote this poem.
Shortly before his death, he requested that I read it out at his funeral.
It was one of the hardest and most beautiful moments of my life.

16 MOTHER'S VENOM

I'm trying to be the bigger person.
But that doesn't really work when.
I've had years of trying and feeling worthless.
Crying into my pillow and feeling hopeless.
I still feel like a child.
When she's bitter and unkind.
Can't tell you how much I've cried.

Her words, the same as they were years ago.
Now, as memories resurface, it only feels like yesterday.
Winding my way through the minefield of mind-fucks and old scars, which stop me from raising the bar and healing.
When I'm still reeling from the last row.
"You're a stupid little bitch and a horrid little cow!"

How could she treat me like that when I was small?
Wasn't she supposed to lift me up?
Not kick me, when I'd fall?
Still makes my blood boil.
Even with a new hope, she spoils.
Everything I want to believe about myself, she foils.
Spitting venom and hate.
And any hope of reconciliation dissipates.
Even though I'm trying to give her a clean slate.

She's still mean and it still grates.
I hate this feeling, but
It's just the state of play.
And I can't seem to find a way to forgive her.
I just want to be able to hug her. And mean it.

I didn't want to give up.
Told myself time and again, I've got to fix up.
Don't feel like she will ever really see the
Magic and the marvel of the real ME.
The one she never understood and still just can't
see.
Disappointment reigns and filters deep.
But the less I speak to her is only faking light relief.

It's never gonna be the way I ever saw it.
She's never gonna be the mum she should've
been.
Too late for that fate.
So what do I do now?
Walk away or stay and bow-down knowing,
In her eyes I just won't be good enough?
But that's too tough to hold on to. And now she's
getting older.
But is my heart really getting colder?

Again and again, I hope for the best.
Hope she'll reach out and try HER best for a change.
Ha! I won't hold my breath.
Guess I'll try again another day.
When I'm ready? Maybe.

Coz I'm trying to be the bigger person.
But that doesn't really work when...
She never liked me in the first place.
Jealousy written all over her face.
Tired of being second place.
Not my fault, I was just a baby.
Still thought one day, she might love me, maybe.

Years of seeking her approval,
Every success I had was futile.
Even when I won, it was meaningless.
When he took my innocence, I was thirteen.
I had to keep it a secret, as no-one would believe
me.
As the shame and disgust coursed through me.
No-one to tell, or he would put it on me, and deny
it.
Make it my fault. So, I zipped-up and kept quiet.
Never to remember 'til I was able.

But what do you do with that information?
Buried so deep, then "pow" a revelation!
Pennies dropping so fast, but not from heaven.
Just reaffirming the secret hell I'd been living.

Realisations and explanations of situations.
And the complications, I'd gone through.
All because of his relationship with you.
Couldn't tell you then, you wouldn't believe it.
Would have called me a shit-stirring bitch.
Nothing new!

But now it's me who's turned the table.
Older and wiser and willing.
To face the abusive hidden demons.
Watch them fester in their hatred.
Now my mutilation spurs my vengeance.
But that's not really me, hence
My desperate need for happiness.
No more venom and duress.
So I ponder my forgiveness and
I wonder...

As the dementia takes hold will she remember?
Even now I'm still trying to do my best for her.

'Cause I'm trying to be the bigger person.
But that doesn't really work when...
We keep going round in circles.
Will she ever feel me in her heart?

So here we are... right back at the start.
No further forward.
And life still hasn't taught her
To see the wonder of her daughter.

18 May 2016

17 FOR KARMELLE

I listened to Karmelle, live at Hysteria.
She was saying she'd cried a river.
She was talking about depression.
And I was remembering every lesson
I've been trying to learn as I go along in life.
And she was right.

She was saying "Life must go on."
So, with every turn of the axis, every word resonated.
As every one of my burnt fingers, from every relationship
That turned from love into hatred
Started throbbing.
I felt it.
Her pain.
Then I thought.
"How come I can't project, like she did?"
Stood on that stage, with her beautiful rage.
Standing tall and looking at you all.

Then I remembered ...
Oh yeah... I've tried so hard to forget my past
I can't even remember the words I write.
'Cause I'm so busy fighting to forget every failure
I've ever been.
So, when you see me up here, reading from my
screen.
Don't judge me, please.

It's because I've still got so much to say, I can't
get away
From the paper and the screen and the words
all float away from me.
Now, I'm not making excuses. She just got my
creative juices going.
And I couldn't get my laptop open quick enough,
'cause the words just kept flowing.

I want to stand here and be good at this thing.
This "spoken word" thing.
If I can touch just one person. Help one person.
Inspire someone.
Like she inspired me to sit and write this?
Then maybe, well, maybe. I'm doing okay.

I listened to Karmelle live at Hysteria.
She was saying she'd cried a river.
She was talking about depression.
But boy, did she make an impression on me?

8 May 2014

18 I'D LIKE TO SHARE MY ADVENTURES WITH YOU

My adventures, so far, are pretty outrageous.
But it seems like I haven't done anything for ages.
I've paddled in the sea in Bognor Regis.
But do you really want to hear about all this?

I've gone crabbing and rock-pooling in Anglesey.
And on school hols it was a race to see who could see the sea.
I've been rained-on in a dingy in Hayling Island.
And sat drinking real Guinness with the locals in Ireland.

I've had fish and chips on the Isle of Wight
And walked up the Champs Elysee at night.
I've seen every castle in Wales, climbed up Snowdon.
I've played arcade games on the pier in Brighton.

I've picked daisies and fed Lavender the Cow in Lime Regis.
I've seen the café where Brad Pitt meets Thelma and Louise.

I've been on a pedalo in España, watched a matador kill a bull.
And eaten more Paella, even though I was full.

I learned to dive in a villa pool in Spain.
To hold my breath and do somersaults, till I was in pain.
I've skied down mountains in Italy, Austria and France.
And I tried to Snowboard in Tahoe (but oof, not a chance).

I've gambled in the Bellagio and the MGM Grand.
And I've walked the strip and Hollywood Boulevard.
I've driven through Turkey in a battered old jeep.
I've had mud baths, seen Geysers and run after sheep.

I've white-water-rafted in Snake River, Wyoming.
And pitched at tent in Yellowstone looking for Yogi.
Back then I never thought about the dangers.
Lucky for me, I only ever saw the Park Rangers.

I've mountain-biked in Telluride and hiked the Grand Canyon.
I've watched Bison lock horns as I've sat by the roadside.
I've ridden with Native Americans through Monument Valley.
I rode like a cowboy; so fast and so free.

I've chased turtles in Dalyan, had too much tequila on a boat.
Woken by the call to prayer, covered in mosquitoes.
I've lain, counting stars with friendly strangers on sand dunes.
It was in Ottawa, in Canada, that I had my first tattoo.

I've trekked around Jenny Lake, where I saw a snake.
Sung "Rocky Mountain High, Colorado", while I was actually there.
(Crikey, I really wish I had seen that bear).
I've sun-bathed on Santa Monica beach and got stoned in South Carolina.
And then fell over coz I'd had too many shots of Goldschlager.

I've seen the sun set through the red rocks of Arches National Park.

I've stayed on someone's private island, skinny-dipped in the dark.

I've snorkeled in The Maldives and swum with a Manta Ray.

Sung "On the road again" when we were all on our way.

I've eaten some of the best cuisine in the world.

Even captured the image of a beautiful Hummingbird.

I've watched people hustle and bustle in the markets of Hong Kong.

Handbags and Frogs, Pak Choy, Dragons and Gongs.

I've quaffed cocktails in San Francisco.

And I've stayed at the Beverley Hills Hotel.

I've danced with ecstasy, in nearly every club in Ibiza.

Watched the Christians and Moors parade at a Fiesta.

I've wandered with romance through the Gothic Quarter.
Been mesmerized by a gypsy guitarist in Barcelona.
I've seen the Mona Lisa in Paris at Le Louvre.
And been up the Eiffel Tower to see the rest of the view.

I've been on the Eurostar to Brussels and eaten waffles
Drenched in Belgian chocolate (so sickly it was awful).
I've sat by the River in Seville, eating calamari.
And stole a doorknob from the Sultan's Palace in Abu Dhabi.

I've been in a glass-bottom boat with a woman in St Lucia.
She had so many braids in her hair, she looked like Medusa.
Done the Limbo with the locals and fell on the floor laughing.
I've been to Verona, in Italy; sightseeing and dancing.

I've been paragliding and thought I was going to die.
Then drunk so much rum punch that I wanted to die.
I've been diamond shopping and stroked camels in Dubai.
And I've looked down from an aircraft to the sea from the sky.

I've water-skied in Lake Powell, saw a scorpion and screamed.
I've ridden the Buffalo Bill roller coaster and screamed.
I've done Yoga at dawn in Marrakech.
Hiked the Atlas Mountains, not sure which way to go next.

I've haggled for cinnamon sticks and rose oil in Morocco.
Been shouted at by Spaniards, "Oi Chica, yo Loco?"
I've seen belly dancers, Flamenco dancers and all manner of
Circus prancers; all amazing and unbelievable sights.

I've had Hammams and Josés and drunk all sorts of Rosés.
Flown First Class and Business and Coach when I need to.
I've been on buses and tubes and the Metro in China.
On bicycles, horses and fancy boats too.
But there are so many things I STILL want do.

I can't really complain though, so far, so good....
Right?
I just hope I have time for the rest.
And I hope you'll really want to hear about that too.

Because I've really enjoyed sharing my adventures with you.

April 2014

19 EIVISSA TE QUIERO (IBIZA I LOVE YOU)

As I sit at a beach bar, the sun on my face.
I remember how much I adore this place.
So many memories, so many good times.
We all have a special place, and well, this is mine.
Every year, since way back when.
(When I was younger and still a size ten).
I've danced on the beaches and in nearly every club.
The daylight never threatening my fun.
I've carried on no matter what.
With not a care to make me stop.
I've double-dropped on Bora Bora.
And never worried about tomorrow.
I've 'come up' on the terrace in Space.
And took a chair in Pacha, just in case.
Sa Trincha, Salinas and Es Cavalet.
Too many to mention, and a few I forget.
So many parties, clubs and dos.
Manumission, Es Vivé, Space, il Ayun.
I've had cocktails and tapas in St José.
Been to Amnesia closing and danced the night away.

Even now, I still feel the draw.
Of this magical island, which still offers more.
Now though, it's all a little more chilled.
No more chasing parties or dragons, and thrills.
Now just the sound of the waves is cool.
Or simply relaxing with a drink by the pool.
But never in my life, will I ever forget.
The times I've had here and I have no regrets.
They all are beautiful parts of my story so far.
And now, I'm quite happy to sit in a bar.
Absorbing the smells, the sights and the sounds.
Reflective and grateful and feeling profound.
But the best part is watching the new people come.
Not realizing the magic they've stumbled upon.
I will always love this fantastic White Isle.
It is full of my mischief, my laughter and smiles.
It's a magical island, no matter your age.
Eivissa te quiero, please don't ever change.

27 April 2014

20 I CAN'T BELIEVE THE AGE I AM

I can't believe the age I am.
I guess I thought things would be different by now.
I've walked up the aisle (twice actually).
Both of those relationships ended quite badly.

You see I grew up believing I would be someone's Mum.
Never thinking for a minute that a child wouldn't come.
Not for the want of trying, that IVF was a pain.
With racing hormones, even faster than Usain.

I've watched suns set on lives, which ended too soon.
I've watched stars align and I've prayed to the moon.
I've skied down mountains and tripped on pavements.
Been beaten, abused and felt utter enragement.
At life and how cruel sometimes it can be.
I've felt the sting of a man's hands on me.

I can't believe the age I am.
I guess I thought things would be different by now.
Being held in the arms of that special someone.
I've cried on my knees, with a pain so intense.
That nothing could help me, no recompense.
Sometimes it all just doesn't make sense.
Life, is hard sometimes and platitudes don't help.

"Be the change you want to see".
"Laugh and the whole world will laugh with me?"
But what about the times when I cry with fear?
The times when loneliness is far too near?
Where is the world then; are they crying with me?
When I sit alone in the dark at night.
And wonder how I STILL get up to fight.

I can't believe the age I am.
I guess I thought things would be different by now.
"It could always be worse" – people say, and they're right.

And on reflection, I've actually done quite a lot in my life.

But I still, can't believe the age that I am.

And I really DID think that things would be different by now.

But maybe, I'm exactly where I need to be.

And I'm not supposed to have done ANYTHING differently.

6 May 2104

21 BEING AN EMPATH

When you feel everything, it's a word they call "EMPATHETIC".
As I watch people's lives crumble, as they stumble along their way.
I cry for them.
That doesn't make me pathetic. Does it?
It makes me sad to see an abused, abandoned donkey or baby.
And I search my soul to see if there is any way that I can help.
Just maybe, I can make a difference, instead of turning away with indifference because we all feel so helpless and consumed in our own processes.
Are we too small to make a change?
Are we so full of fear and dread that our voices are too small?
So, when you feel this thing called EMPATHY, and you stand by when someone's sanity is threatened.
With every child that's slain by a bullet too soon, or a community ravaged by a tsunami or monsoon.
I cry.

When guns are wielded, bullets fired.
When sons and daughters, mothers and men are slaughtered.
Ask yourself why?
STAND UP!
Open your heart; show your tears and cry.
Feel that passion for the right thing, and rise.
Say NO. Say STOP! Because to challenge is ALL we've got.
Feel empathy and kindness.
Ask yourself is there something I can do, or someone I can write to?
Sign a petition, hold a concert, bake a cake and run for your life to end this repetition.
Destruction of our trust is in full swing.
Whilst governments and politicians spin.
The truth is theirs and they believe that what they feed us feeds OUR needs.
But it doesn't.
Sincerity is lost these days.
Platitudes and lip service from the media.
Create a false belief and hope, which quickly fades.
Commercials lie, conglomerates buy, stocks and shares go high and we don't know how to live with love and compassion anymore.

Got to have more, buy more, get more, see more, need more, more, more, MORE.

And it stings my eyes and makes my heart and SOUL sore.

What we really need is empathy, alacrity and honesty.

Not APATHY...

So when you feel that tug at your heartstrings, let yourself feel it.

Bask in its discomfort, then build on it and reel it in,

to push you.

Make someone believe in you.

Stand up for something better, truer.

I feel everything – always have.

Because I'm an EMPATH.

Being EMPATHETIC doesn't make me pathetic.

It makes me sensitive and kind and sadder than you will ever know...

Because I feel everything in the world that's wrong and bad... with every fiber of my being.

I have to shut my eyes to stop them seeing, sometimes.

So this is my prayer: -

Put the guns down.
Pick a child up.
Feed the homeless.
Set an animal free.
STOP LYING TO ME.
Put. The. Guns. Down.
And make peace.
Please.

So maybe all of us sensitive souls, can get a good nights sleep.

November 2016

22 ROUND AND ROUND

Shall I share, can I speak?
When everything that comes out of my mouth just wreaks of the past mistakes and the weakness of bad judgements and young blunders which I stand by, but hold inside?
All this makes up the woman I am now.
So how can I deny the glory and the tragedies I've endured to get to this version of me?
Hopefully he'll get me, and still want to protect me.
So here we go.
As I ride on time,
Step-by-step and try once again to stand next to someone else.
As another man holds my hand and takes a stand.
On the fight to win my heart.
Round and round we go. Take a step forward and reach,
Trying not to breach the rules of this engagement.
A new encounter.
With witty banter and sideways glances.
Wondering if this is just another peacock dance.
Or is this real romance?
Seems so long, I can't remember the last time someone was cleverly tender with his game.

He seems to be trying hard.
But I'm on my guard
And it's hard for him to crack my shell.
Don't want to show and tell too soon.
I want him to touch the dial and tune in on my wavelength.
Show me some courage and strength.
But still be gentle with his needs and not pander too much.
And not meander nor push either.
Neither of us are sure what's real anymore.
Questions, probing, quizzing, talking 'til we're dizzy.
And just wanting that connection; the "click" that we're in the vicinity of finding that divinity of the perfect pair.
With firm belief that they're out there somewhere.
And this could work.
Couldn't it?
He's sweet and nervous, gentle and reserved.
But still showing enough strength to keep me intrigued.

But, are we even in the same league?
Do we want the same things and where will it lead?
Chill babe and breath...
Date number three; Sunday lunch, perhaps a walk in the park and a kiss maybe?
Don't know yet.
Guess we'll Just have to wait and see.

16 October 2015

23 FOR KARL

My friend Karl wrote on Facebook:

"I made two new friends this weekend, they were sisters in fact, 'Saturday Morning & Sunday Morning. Apparently, I met them years ago on a few occasions, but I was always with World of Pain and her evil twin Walk of Shame and together, well, they don't all really get on... I really hope I see them again for many more weekends to come, for they are actually, beautiful."

And it inspired me to write this:

GOTTA STOP THIS SHIT SOON

So wrapped up in the drama.

Fun bus, record spins, club to club, we're chasing hits...
Gotta stop this shit soon.

Rack up a line, drink some wine, party on we'll be fine, keep on going, toxic fuel is flowing we'll be fine... yeah, I'll take a break soon.

Thursday night, drinks after work, off to a club, music loud, "twerk"!
Lay in bed till five or six, get up and start again, clubbing friends, record spins, take a pill...
Gotta stop this shit soon.

Friday – How? Can't stop now, we're rolling into Saturday and Sunday now the party's on a Monday. Bank Holiday, chill out bruv skin up a J... Yeah, don't worry, cuz. Gotta stop this shit soon.

Next stop, down a shot, where next? After-party no-one rests, off we go, it started Thursday, but now it's Tuesday morning. Shit!
Now we've really gotta stop this shit soon.

Wednesday back to work, only one day to go before we start again, take a shot, bring the drama, fun bus, record spins, club to club we're chasing hits... SURELY we've gotta stop this shit soon?

Finally, you take a break, everything is starting to shake, girl's make-up looking like cake, can't eat, body, face, teeth and jaw all ache... Stop... and breathe!

Oh... Saturday morning – so this is what you look like.
Damn!

11 May 2014

24 POLITICS

Now, I haven't got a clue when it comes to matters of the nation.
I read leaflets in stations and some of what I read makes me stop in my tracks.
So I stand still.

I'm stationary as their glossy stationery feeds lies into me.
Racism, journalism, idealism and every facet of non-realism.
Drips like a faucet, forcing me to decide where I lie.
But I can't decide. I'm supposed to vote – but for who?

Local politicians, who I have no recollections of even knowing
Who are they?
How can I decide if what they say is even growing my community, with immunity and no purity that I can see.
No truths, no genuine concerns, just lyrical twisting and spinning by the spin-doctors that make what they say fit in to your day.
Putting words in my mouth.
Hearing myself shout stuff I don't even believe in.

I can't believe the words I'm hearing.
All I'm seeing is the fear they're instilling.
So I stand still.

I'm stationary, as their glossy stationery feeds lies into me.
Racism, journalism, sexism and every facet of non-realism
Drips like a faucet, forcing me to decide where I lie.

But I can't decide. I'm supposed to vote – but for who?
I've got to make a decision based on someone else's vision
Of long division of numbers and facts so convoluted
It doesn't matter if I live in Kensington or Tooting.
So what do I do?

Who are these people, telling me how I should be?
I don't know them. I don't trust them.
So I stand still.

I listen to the news; to the way 'they' want it portrayed.
That's not really how it is, we're not given the full story.
But as the newsreaders bask in their TV fame and glory.
Do they know what they are doing, by making a mockery of the truth?
No.
So I stand still.

I'm stationary, as their glossy stationery feeds lies into me
Sexism, racism, idealism and every facet of non-realism
Drips like a faucet, forcing me to decide where I lie.
But I can't decide.

I've got to make a decision. I've got to vote.
But I haven't got a clue!

Although I know what I'd like to do.
I'd like to vote for HONESTY and the TRUTH.

How about you?

8 May 2014

25 EARLY DAYS

As interest blossoms, newly forming.
Heart races when you think he's phoning.
Texts a plenty, fresh as morning.
Building tension, games we're honing.
Feel that frisson in the air.
Early days, so taking care.
Bringing out your A game – true.
Need to show the best of you.
Laughing, breezy, chilled and cool,
Making jokes and playing the fool!
Check my phone in case I miss you.
Beep beep - message coming thru!
And so the games begin once more.
Interest heightens, wanting more.
How to act in circumstance.
A change for both, as time has passed.
Anticipating first days kiss.
Hoping for that scorching bliss.
Early days must take it slow.
Gently does it, innit tho!
Get to know what makes him tick.
See if you will get that "click".

Interest blossoms, he calls again.
His obvious intent sustains.
Hanging up you feel that smile.
Haven't felt this for a while.
As interest heightens, nerves ascend.
Will this be the one to break the trend?
Raise the bar and take the chance.
Move away from timid stance and
Welcome this new circumstance.
Gently does it, soft and slow as.
His intent rocks me to and fro.
So come on in, it's been a while.
He kisses me, and I watch him smile.

21 July 2012

26 THE MEN IN MY LIFE

The first man I ever knew was my Dad.
He was the best man I have EVER known.

The next was my brother – he didn't like me.
We don't even speak now. He was rude and abused me.

The first man I slept with, he beat me and raped me.

The first man I really loved, he cheated on me.

The first man I married, used me for money.

The first man to call me 'friend', he wanted more.

They all promise the world and deliver the curb!

What lessons I learned from these men in my life?

Let's see...

The second man I married - I cheated on him.

Now I sleep with them, before I call them 'friend'.

I distrust their motives before I give them a chance.
But I still go along with the "relationship" dance.

So you see my encounters with men are pretty fucked.

So how to behave with my three new brothers?
Shit!
Wish me luck.

5 March 2014

27 I LOST YOU

He abused me.

Kicked me down the stairs.
'Til I was black and blue.
And you saw it.

He used me.

Six foot four, he knew the score.
I was useless to defend myself.
Again and again.
But you saw it.

He hurt me.

With a level of disrespect you wouldn't expect.
From anyone you loved.
And you saw it.

I hurt you.

Every time I left you to be with him.
And ignore the obvious.
I saw it.

I broke you.

Every time I ended up in your arms.
Because of the harm he'd cause me.
I felt it.

You loved me.

You'd wrap me up in your patience.
Give me a hot mug of caring and wait.
So you waited.

I was weak.

But you were strong enough for both of us.
And held on to your harboured tenderness.
Until I was ready, and then...

He raped me.

Tore at me like a rag doll, fit for the bin.
I came straight to you. I said nothing,
But you knew.

I lost you.

Not used to the level of respect you showed me.
I returned the favour by disrespecting you.

He hurt me.
I hurt you.

He broke me.
But I lost you.

8 April 2014

28 KARMA'S A BITCH

Sometimes I sit in the bathroom and cry.
Hug my knees to my chest and ask myself "Why"?
Why do I feel like the world is against me?
Why do I feel like my Mum never loved me?

Used to dance for her, sing for her, always I'd try.
To get her attention, but it was always denied.
"Stop showing off; go to your room", she'd say.
And so I'd hide and try again another day.

Sometimes I sit in the bathroom and cry.
Hug my knees to my chest and ask myself "Why"?
Told her that my friends brother said he was
gonna rape me.
She slapped me round the face and said
"Stop being a drama queen".

So I didn't dare tell her that YOU made me do
things.
Because you were her favourite. You were her king.
I was thirteen when you made me promise never
to tell.
So I kept it inside and just lived through the hell.
And I sat in the bathroom feeling dirty and sly.
Hugging my knees to my chest asking myself
"Why"?

But now it's my choice to stop asking "Why"?
Now I hold on to my power and hold my head high.
It is what it is, I can now justify.
It could have been worse, so how lucky am I?

Now I look at myself in the mirror and smile.
'Cause Karma's a bitch, but it may take a while.

26 March 2014

29 THE FRIENDSHIP FAIRY

Some have said I'm a Fairy.
Some say a gift from God.
Some say I'm a bit too larey.
And I can be a bit of a sod.

But without my friends, I'm no-one.
They're the ones who give me my spark.
They're the reason I carry on some days.
When I'd be happy to just sit in the dark.

They give me hope when I lose my way.
Tell me the sun WILL come out, just not today.
And when I have good news to share.
I pick up the phone and someone is there.

So you see this Fairy is wistful.
And grateful to all of you guys.
For the moments we have, which are blissful.
And for the days when there are only grey skies.
For the laughter, the memories, the good and
the bad.
For helping me when sometimes I'm just a bit
sad.

So, remember today, as you go your own way.
And as life caries on day-to-day.
That this Friendship Fairy will always be here.
When you need someone to dry YOUR tears.

5 May 2014

30 HE DIDN'T HAVE A PROBLEM – DID HE?

"Shut-up I haven't got a problem." He said. 'It's fine"

Just something he did occasionally, to have a good time.

Said there was always time, to have another line.

It didn't mean anything; he wasn't "that guy".

Just roll up a note and pour us a drink.

"Come on ... let's get wasted." He said.

"Shut-up I haven't got a problem." He said.

He controlled IT, IT didn't control him.

And so he made the call.

As he punched in the number and paced up the hall.

Running his hands through his hair.

A concerned look on his face.

But the guy wasn't there.

The phone rang and rang until it went dead.

"Shut-up I haven't got a problem." He said.

His voice louder now, and with a slight edge.

I just want a bit more, got some shit going on in my head.

Just a little bit – that's all.

"You call; see if he picks up for you" he says.

But it rang and rang until it went dead.

"Shut-up I haven't got a problem." He said.
"Ah man, call the other guy, he'll be around.
I'll go to him; he's probably in town".
As he dials the number, he frowns.
And bead of sweat on his forehead drips down.
He's shouting now and he slams down the phone.
'Cause it rang and rang until it went dead again.

"Shut-up I haven't got a problem." He said.
"I'm leaving now – don't worry, I'm tired".
I'm ready for bed now, but he's really wired.
He's frothing and angry and racking his brain.
Who can he call to get some cocaine?
His eyes widen in realisation.
There's a bloke he knows down by the station.

"Shut-up I haven't got a problem." He said.
Babe gives us a lift before you go home.
Stay with me and have some more blow.
I'll try him now; will you take me to Soho?
But like Nancy Reagan, I just say "No".
Can't watch him disappear into someone I don't know.

So I kiss him goodnight – 'Look after yourself and just go to bed".
But he has got a problem, hasn't he? I said.
As I speak to his friends and we plan an intervention.
Well, the road to hell is paved with good intentions.
We all know he's gonna hate us for this.
But we can't watch him keep putting himself through this shit.

We didn't hear from him for while after that.
He went on a bender... And then he was dead.
"We didn't realise he was that bad". They said.

2 April 2014

31 I'M CONFUSED

Because when we talk about colour, whether black or white.
I don't understand why there is such a divide.
Let me be clear, I'm not dispelling years of oppression.
And I hate any aggression towards the colour of a person's skin.

I'm confused.
Because when I see colour, I see a multitude of nations.
One people – all the universes' creations.
I love that people celebrate their colour.
But surely, we should ALL celebrate with each other?

I'm confused.
Because when I see a berry black as night, it's a sight to behold.
And when the white crystal snow settles on a branch in the cold.
It's beautiful.

I'm confused.
Because I see bursts of colour in the spring, the blossom on trees,
The grass, the flowers.
I could spend hours just looking and appreciating.
Not hating.

I'm confused.
How history tells tales of colour being abused.
I'm disgusted with the twisted shit that went down.
At the hands of some people. But they're not MY people.

I'm confused.
There are so many grey areas, where really, it should be clear.
We're all here;
We can all hear the haters.
Their ignorance is blatant.
It disgusts me.

I'm confused.
I don't care where you come from, or who you
are.
We've all come this far and now I want to shout
It's not about the black or the white.

It should be about unity.
It should be about us.
It should be about love.
Shouldn't it?

Or am I just confused?

8 April 2104

32 I WANT STEREO

I don't want MONO...I want STEREO, so please. Turn up the BASS and the TREBLE, don't tease.

This GIG is on and I'm reverberating and tuning-in on your level.

It's not a sound check, or a speaker test, microphone teaser.

Get the graphic equalizer set, tune-in and tweak me.

Don't mess with the balance, listen to my talents. I'm on the stage and ready to commit. The audience is waiting.

Anticipating the roar, and the crowd will watch us soar.

I don't want to be bouncing off the walls, while you're in the stalls.

Waiting for the MUSIC to hit your ears. I want to sound you out

Ride on your WAVELENGTH, with a supersonic, quadraphonic headset.

Get set, get ready to go steady and fill the auditorium.

With DECIBELS and SONIC boom, I need our magic to be AUDIBLE.

You'll still feel my resonance when the lights are off.

Your eyes speak volumes, but is it enough?

Our music needs clarification. So sharpen up that backing track.

No messing around with the support act. I AM the main feature.

No ProTools manipulation here, just pure sound engineer-ing.

No in and out phasing here... just ease me in with an 8 bar intro.

I don't want to stand still, I want to move my DANCIN' feet.

Mix it in and drop that BEAT, feed the RHYTHM and turn up the heat.

You've given me the HOOK, now set the TEMPO.

Let's go, baby coz I'm your White Label hit and here's the spin-back.

Slip me onto your turntable and hear the RIFF on this new track.

I'm high quality WAV (not a WAG) and I won't let up.

I've got all the equipment ready and set-up.

LISTEN to the words I write and HEAR this message tonight.

Loud and clear like fine-tuned sound. I was lost. But now I'm found.

This is my pitch... I'm your (new) unusual melody.

I'm not just a jingle baby – I'm The Whole Symphony.

No strings attached no brass or tack, but baby I've got your back.

I'm your Gospel Choir and what I require is a beautiful HARMONY.

But YOU'RE the one conducting me.

So with soul and funk even opera too. I just want to sing with you.

I don't want MONO...I want STEREO.

So baby, don't tease. Turn up the BASS AND the TREBLE.

Please.

2 February 2015

33 I STILL BELIEVE

People say "be careful what you wish for."
In a world where no-one's sure of anything anymore.
'Cause what you might get, is not what it seems.
But I still believe HE'S out there. The Butch to my Cassidy.
And we will dance in the sun. He WILL be the one.
I'm 'a find him someday and he's gonna make my head sway.
I'm 'a keep on keeping on, keep on movin' don't stop now.
I'm 'a find that WOW Factor, that X Factor.
Somewhere's Got Talent, with a fast-track to what I want.
I wanna hear his footsteps on my dance floor.
When he's killing me softly with his lips of gold.
And holding me tenderly, when we get old and Grey, he'll stay and we'll laugh out loud and still, play the music loud.
We'll lay in the grass and watch the clouds just pass us by.
Stroking face and hair, the time will fly, we'll talk and share.
He'll be Easy, Like a Sunday Morning and There IS No Mountain High Enough, this is my warning.

I'm 'a find him... The Man I Love.
The promise of him will keep me warm.
The memories of love that's gone. The life I lead still, goes on.
But I still believe that he's out there.
Like Beyonce to JZ, and Bill Compton to Suki.
Like Scarlett to Rhett... I'll still believe until I'm dead.
It'll be the best romance novel, like Mills and Boon.
A love so strong it WILL consume.
So while I'm resting with you a while.
Take your time to laugh and smile.
Life is short but hopes and dreams keep us alive, or so it seems.
Daydreams, wistful thoughts and hopes,
do not steal away in a midnight elope.
I am steadfast strong, tenacious and our union WILL be delicious.
Like a cherry on the icing. Swipe your finger through the taste of me.
A sample of what's yet to come.
I'm 'a be the Kir in your Royale.
Dive in deep, no shallow-end here.
My rivers run dark with bubbles and 'bends'.

Your blood will boil and then descend.

I'll blow your mind, then kiss you better.

Like Romeo and Juliet, but with a death-defying end.

Like Marilyn and JFK but this time, the heroine will stay.

My Tarzan, to your Jane.

My prince, he'll come, when it's least expected.

It could be you, or it could be the next man.

But... Just so long as you know.

I'm 'a keep on going till I find him.

Then I'm gonna love him, cherish him and hold him.

Coz I still believe... Yep, I STILL believe that you're out there.

Somewhere.

And when I do find you.

Then I'm gonna sing

"You're my first, my last, my everything".

10 July 2014

34 THE COLOURS OF LIFE

Emerald lawns and turquoise seas.
The black and yellow of honeybees.
White, fluffy clouds and hazelnut eyes.
The violet hews of a perfect night sky.
The mirrored-blue tint of Ray Bans.
And the orangey tinge of a St Tropez tan.
These are all the colours of life.

Pink, freckled noses.
The deep red of Love roses.
Blonde, curly beach hair.
A brown grizzly bear.
The purple of crocuses signaling Spring.
The shining silver of a friendship ring.
These are all the colours of life.

A tall, dark, handsome fella.
Sipping a cold, liquid gold Stella.
An ivory bride as she walks down the aisle.
Those old, green wellies you haven't worn in a
while.
Terracotta pots in the garden all stacked.
And a paisley wool rug, full of dust, being wacked.
These are all the colours of life.

The light speckled coral of a fresh lobster tail.
The crystal-clear shine of a small garden snail.
A child's face after they've eaten ice cream.
And when they fall over, their little purple knees.

The comforting sight of paramedic green.
And the bright white of bleach when you know
something's clean.

These are all the colours of life, it seems.
So how come it's all black and white when we
dream?

30 April 2014

35 SOMEONE'S MUM

I always believed I'd be someone's Mum.
Have a little life grow in my tum.
Watch my baby suck her thumb.
But now, now I just feel numb.

All curly, blonde hair and loving smiles.
Pigtails, ladybirds and ice creams.
Big blue eyes looking up at me.
Filled with wonder, possibility and dreams.
But sadly, that was not for me.

It's a miscarriage of justice.
IVF and Gonal F,
Daily injections met with
Measured doses of hope and dread.
My vision of how things could have gone.
Was it my fault, or what did I do wrong?

The "what if's" and "when she comes".
I'll love her more than anyone.
I'll be her Mum.
Never make the mistakes mine did.

The love I have inside me.
Still hasn't reached its full capacity.
Maybe that's why it suffocates all the men I see.
(That's probably why they leave me)!

It's all consuming.
To love a child.
That love knows no bounds.
I have nowhere else to direct it, see.
Except my furry family.
My friends and my newly found siblings, three.
But they're not that special part of me.
I always believed I'd have with me.
My little girl, my tomboy, climbing trees.
Grazing knees and running to Mummy.
For first aid reassurance.
Distracting her with something funny.
To dry the tears and make her laugh.
Splash about at bedtime bath.
Sing her to sleep and pray to keep her safe.
To make sure she's alive when I awake.

But alas.

Not for me, this path of motherhood.

Now menopause has ended all hope.

Deep emotions circle and choke.

The inhalation of this reality smoke.

Is sometimes too much for even me to cope with.

Because I always believed I'd be someone's Mum.

2 October 2017

36 A TRIBUTE TO FRANKIE KNUCKLES

A Legend of House Music, died yesterday.
I was one of the lucky ones.
I heard him play.

He delved into samples of funky soul train.
Brought us up on our feet dancin'
Again and again.

Our music was House, and he was the Master.
Got us grooving together, like no other
task-master.
But his task was fierce. His disciples, all fearless.
As we danced to his tunes and each sing-out-
loud chorus.

The dance floor was buzzing, the bass coming
through.
Frankie knew how to lure us when he dropped
a tune.
It was fat and full-blooded, like a full fruity wine.
He'd tease us, then hit us and the drop was
sublime.

Angelic soul divas, with voices of honey.
Goosebumps and shivers, butterflies in our
tummies.

As the crescendo kept rising, we all tagged
along.
And raised our hands in the air to our own special
song.

Well our hands are up now. But we're waving
goodbye.
To the Master of House Music, and it's our
"Tears" that cry.

Goodbye Frankie and thank you, it won't the
same.
Hear our "Tears" on the dance floor, and play it
again.

R.I.P. Frankie Knuckles
18 January, 1955 to 31 March, 2014

1 April 2014

37 THE YO YO RAP

Put your hands in the air like you just don't care.
Stevie-Boo's in the house and you'd better beware.
With curves like Jessica, she's more than a rabbit.
Got a thirst for the fast Layne and a Selfridges habit.
She's hanging in the hood, but she's keeping it breezy.
Watch how she works it, she makes it look easy.
She's keeping it real, one day at a time.
Running through the streets, but this lady's no grime.
It's hard going solo, but she's making her money.
"Let's Face It" together; she's a real sweet honey.
Got a heart of gold, that she'll share if you're nice.
Don't f*&k with her boy, yeah, you'd better think twice.
She's sweet like candy, you better believe it.
Mess up her whip and you'll certainly feel it.
She floats like a butterfly and stings like a bee.
Bend over baby and get down on your knees.
She's a puppy-loving lady, but no dogging please.

No wandering around naked in the trees, this lady.
She's up from the country, but now London's her home.
But the world is her oyster; she's got the will to roam.
Paris, Ibiza, London, Milan.
But palm trees and oceans is really the plan.
Laying on the sand with her man on the beach.
Not long now, but how are you gonna reach?
Put your foot on the gas, 'cause we're going full speed.
No slowing down or chilling out on the weed.
Take it or leave it, this girl's gonna bust.
If you can't take the heat boy, then you'd better just duss.

2015

38 AN ODE TO BALLS

What Happens Below the Belt?

In the process of grooming, don't leave out your balls.
For they're the giver of life, they produced us all.
Those spherical love eggs, just under your tummy.
Covered in chicken skin, odd shaped and funny,
Dangling there like a bad after thought.
Time to fix-up, get them all smooth and taught.
Freshen them up with Waterless Cleanser.
It's not rocket science and there's no need for Mensa.
Sat on and squeezed-in, chaffed-up and left out.
Get some Sports Lube on them, let the Testie come out!
Slaver them, massage them, freshen, protect.
Below The Belt Products, will aid in your trek.
Climbing or boxing, cycling, running or fishing.
Look after your balls; they're the gift that keeps giving!

13 February 2016

39 NO PROMISES, DEMANDS OR DIAMONDS REQUIRED

Can't put my finger on it, but I have no choice.
Can't rest my bones without hearing your voice.
I just need to hear that you're okay.
And I wanna hear all about your day today.

When we're close, it works and I see where you're coming from.
No need to hide from this girl, so stop all that running Fam.
Listen to the beat and hear with your heart.
And ask yourself why's it so hard when we're apart?

You say you don't have time to waste on lies.
But I get nervous when we say our goodbyes.
You've got your stuff to do and I've got mine.
You say don't worry Boo, it's all cool and you're fine.

Then I call and you don't pick up.
I wonder what's going on and what could be up.
When we talk it seems you misunderstood.
Thinking I've done something that I never would.

I know you've been hurt, but I'm something new.
Please leave her in the past and push away those blues.
If I was your daughter, you'd tell me to leave it.
And give my love to someone else, who deserves it.

But when I say I'm leaving, you tell me it's not what you meant.
Saying you don't want me to go, but my heartstrings are spent.
You make me dangle; I'm dizzy from all the to-ing and fro-ing.
One day I'm staying, the next day I'm going.

You say you miss me when I'm not there.
That I'm lovely and gorgeous and of course you care.
You say you're not my boyfriend, coz you need to remember
How to trust again and to give your heart to surrender.

I understand what you're saying and I'm not in a hurry.
So please take it easy and stop with the flurry.
Can't keep up with the switches, you're up and you're down.
Wanna keep the smile on my face and stop with the frowns.

Listen boy, this is how I feel.
Just need you to keep this shit real.
Don't get yourself into such a confused state.
I am patient and kind and willing to wait.

Enjoy the good when the good times roll.
Don't let your past keep taking its toll.
Open up slowly and just let it rain.
Wash away the heartache, the tears and the pain.

Dance in the daylight, look up to the sun.
Bask in the moment and come have some fun.
There's no agenda, no fight, I'm a genuine girl.
I wanna make you laugh; I wanna rock your world.

Baby steps, gently, that's all I desire.
No promises, demands or diamonds required.

25 September 2014

40 HOLIDAY ROMANCE

Such a cliché, "The Holiday Romance"!
An unexpected chance encounter forming.
Full moon, lightening, stormy skies and shooting
stars.
Beach bars and lazy summer days.
Stealing glances as eyes meet across the way.

The magic continues through the night.
Those duplicated smiles of delight and
That tilt of possibilities which might
Be something worth exploring.
(Something more than UK boring).

No time to waste, so let's dive in.
Chemical burst surprises in a beautiful strangers'
kiss.
Long and lingering moments of unadulterated
bliss.
Locking eyes and lips, then hips.

We're on slo-mo, Cherry Mojitos flow and no
work restraining.
Memories of past trashy novels painting
pictures of the perfect romantic situation.

Whilst on vacation from a life you left behind.
Maybe only for a weekend or even a fortnight.
So we take it in our stride with no worries, constraints or pride.

The game's afoot but everyone's winning,
Heads spinning in the seemingly perfect moment.
Sizzling hot excitement rises.
Heart quickens, blood pulses and nothing matters.
Except this melting moment of happiness.

Fools rush in with romantic daydreams.
Swimming in the slipstream of possibilities that linger and taunt.
Carefree days, not much to report,
Only now the nights are just too short.

No sleep required even though we're tired.
Every second counts, no jumping sheep.
Just wrapping feet entwined in sheets.

But when he treats you like there's no one else there.
Like you're the one he's waited for?
An Angel in a devil's lair.
Faking feelings, which seem real there.
Pick and mix bikini shows.
New blood daily - nothing stays
Or sustains...
But who dares wins - right?

Shall I stay just one more night? Why not?
Nothing to lose until it's gone.
Flights changed, ecstasy and agony, both prolonged.
Goodbyes now even harder as normality bites and groans.
But if you take that chance
Will you remember?
It's just a holiday romance?
Or was it?

Landing home with a hard bump of misery.
Holiday blues, or are you just missing him?
Hard to tell but when the phone rings, it's him.
How do you feel now?
Was it a dream or is he real?
Saying words he thinks he's meaning.
Fantasies, romantic dreaming.

In that second, do you believe him and steal that
thought?
Or just put it down to experience.
Get a grip and get on with it.

Memories of him still so fresh.
The urgent passion of his kiss.
Will take me through the next few weeks until...
I book my flight to go back again.
But days go by and his number gets further
down the WhatsApp message list.
Those blistering kisses, now misty memories.
Oh well. I guess... It is what it is.
Nothing more and now, so much less.
Than simply this.
A Holiday Romance.

8 August 2017

41 WHAT YOU SEE IS WHAT YOU GET?

If you should look at me and like.
What meets your eyes both up and down.
Remember what you get inside.
Is not always what you see just now.

For I can be so many things.
In thought and mind and deed.
And if you love the way I am.
Remember I can change to be.

Something else if you should wish.
Or stay the same, so do you see.
That what you see is what you get.
But maybe not - just wait and see!

March 1996

42 LIFE

I wonder when the end will come, the silent peaceful sleep.
To rid the harsh and hurtful times. Why do I sit and weep?
Behind my smile, my cheery face. Behind the curtains drawn.
My sadness grew beyond control, and others now will mourn.

How could I be so lonely, with friends who loved me so?
They never really knew the hurt, and why I have to go.
So sad to leave my lover, I long to comfort him.
I know he really loves me, but goodbye to love - and him.

Their tears begin to slowly fall, for now the party's over.
Time to clear up all the mess, for I have now passed over.
Too late to save me, now I'm gone - I've left the hurt behind.
Though self-inflicted silently, I smile a peaceful smile.

Confusion, hate and torment and stifled cries and sobs.
The question - Why of everything, is Life the hardest job?

3 August 1993

43 CROUCH

As he squirms and spits, his venom stings.
His twisted frame, head low, exhibiting.
His paranoia, it looms and seeps.
As he sniffs it under the rug and sweeps.
If only he could stop his fight.
Against love and friendship in daylight.
When darkness falls as he awakes.
Perpetuating his mistakes.
Round and round his groundhog day.
Pushes good stuff far away.
Reaching for his trusty herb.
He slips off yet another curb.
Walk the walk alone and trust
No one – he thinks he has it sussed.
Chip away at someone good.
Disrespectful, nasty, rude.
Push away, try to control.
Sniff some more he's on a roll.
Do the flat up later, yeah?
Tidy up, nah, just don't care.
Round and round his groundhog night.
Call the crack-whores to feed his plight.
Sniff and roll, lug and lurch.
Welcome to the chemical church.

He prays at the alter of yayo rock.
Which keeps him soft and in the dock.
Three blue pills and still no joy.
Don't worry, mate I'll use my toy!
In chemical his stake invested.
Bad taste in his mouth; indigestion.
Can't swallow a word like "normal".
Thinks his lifestyle makes him immortal.
Like MC Hammer, "you can't touch this".
So he walks alone in his ignorant bliss.
One trusty fucked-up drug-fuelled mate.
Better call him, lock the gate.
Who's at the door, how do they know?
Quick let's hide the blow.
Running out, call someone quick.
Roll a joint and take a hit.
Round and round his groundhog day.
No more friends, they've gone away.
Silly fucked up junkie twat.
Nothing left, so I guess that's that!

2013

44 THE STREETS OF MY HOMETOWN

There's nothing quite like driving through the streets of my hometown at night.
3am, no traffic, clear roads and the moon is high.
I even spotted a few stars up in the sky.
Stopped at a shop and a drunken couple give a cursory nod.
Everything is as it should be, right now.
Smiling, and content, I pull up to my house.
There's a parking spot for me, right outside.
Thanks Universe. That's nice.
I'm having a good night tonight.
Make-up off, it's still warm out.
I've had a good day.
Time for bed.
Got a smile on my face and I'm in a good place.
Grateful for the wheels I drive.
Driving around London, free and easy, when I like.
Yeah, there's nothing quite like driving through the streets of my hometown at night.

July 2016

45 THE NEIGHBOURHOOD THESE DAYS

I look around the neighbourhood these days
Someone always looking to get paid.
See a lad in the street, Dre's Beats in his ears.
Rapping bars, spitting lyrics, while he's sipping his beer.

Hoody up for protection from CCTV.
No protection for his girlfriend though, she's pregnant with his kid.
Wondering if he's ever gonna get a break in his life.
And will their kid be a cause of more strife?

This lad who wanted to be an engineer.
Now fights for his family, selling weed and gear.
No-one takes pride in their street anymore.
Robbing and stealing, litter on the floor.

This boy's oozing with talent that nobody sees.
Doors slammed in his face, and he's brought to his knees.

"Send off your demo to our A&R dept please."
A brief taster of fame, but it's only a tease.

Hip-hop and grime, rap, drum n bass.
You can see the disappointment etched on his face.
Forget the system it's useless, corrupt.
His dreams are just laughed at and he's told to shut up.

You can see him writing his life down in lyrics.
Don't blind-side him with a new sheet of statistics.
He's working in Tescos counting and stacking.
Whilst spitting bars faster that Cadbury's can wrap it.

Later he's selling a bar and a quarter.
Just so he can afford to buy clothes for his daughter.
If I could change something in my neighbourhood.
I'd give him an outlet, something to make him feel good.

Give him the tools to make himself heard.
And the belief that his dreams are not at all obsurd.

Give him an opportunity and give him a chance. Bring him on with encouragement, uplift and enhance.

I look around the neighbourhood these days. But today I wish it was this lad getting paid.

29 May 2014

46 MY JOURNEY

Be gentle with me oh wise ones out there.
I am only just learning to love myself.
I still don't know what that means yet.
It is a long road ahead.
Sometimes I will fail and my ego will rage.
And sometimes I will curl up in a ball and cry.
Be gentle with me oh wise ones out there.
For you do not know some of the terrain I have trod.
You can only see what I choose to project.
Some of this however, will not be a choice.
But my past is beckoning me to wallow a while.
I will try to be conscious and hold my head up and smile.
And not repeat past patterns of damage.
Be gentle with me, oh wise ones out there.
For I am still only learning.
And only really yearning for Peace... Serenity....
Silence.
Shelter from the noise that fills my head sometimes.
To be free of the baggage I long to lose.
And the future I long to seize.
Be gentle with me oh wise ones out there.
I am trying, I will falter... But I WILL prevail.

Thank you.

PART TWO

MATES. MENOPAUSE. MISCHIEF.

Welcome to Part Two

It seemed rather fitting that I completed the second part of this compilation, Mates. Menopause. Mischief. In the five years after my first book, Live. Love. Laugh.

What a ridiculous few years we have all had to endure. 2019-2021 was a very strange time indeed. Covid-19, lockdown madness; travel bans and restrictions. I have no idea what to say about that... but there's a poem somewhere in here about it!

So, here it is, my second book; Mates. Menopause. Mischief.

xoxo

ACKNOWLEDGEMENTS
PART TWO

To Mum

This is sadly being written whilst you're losing your life and your mind to dementia, in hospital. Sadly, you'll never see these words in print. You'll never hear the sentiments and hopefully, never really know the extent of pain I have come through. This is my forgiveness to you, for causing so much of that pain. Goodbye Mum, may you finally rest in peace.

Mates

Some have come and some have gone. Some of you are new. But all of you add a richness to my life which I, quite honestly, could not live without.

You are my tribe, my crew. The strong, the steadfast, the loyal; and I'm grateful for each and every one of you. The wheel of life goes around, but real friends will always return. Some of you are featured in here. Thank you for enriching me; you are my gold, my jewels and my diamonds.

Menopause

Probably the worst natural process a woman can go through in her life. Please don't underestimate it. It's hideous. All you chaps, husbands, brothers and fathers, nephews and sons out there... please be understanding, we really are not in charge of our emotions at this time.

Mischief

Anyone who knows me, knows I don't believe in regrets. I make choices and then relish in the lessons I learn from the consequences.
It's not always easy, but no good ever comes from easy.

Finally, and most importantly, I wouldn't change a thing. Anyway... "Life without a little Mischief, is no life at all."

1 MENOPAUSE MADNESS

Who is this person I see in the mirror?
Surely it cannot be me.
Now I have fat in some very strange places.
Now I can't bear what I see.

My skin has changed colour.
My hair is now dry.
My body is doing strange things. I'm moody and
tearful and so bloody fearful;
I cry at the stupidest things.

I'm hot, then I'm cold.
My clothes are all wrong.
My jeans are like jeggings these days.
I'm tired and batty, I've turned into a "fatty".
My youth has turned into a haze.

I take tablets and hormones.
God knows I keep trying.
Tried Vegan and watch what I eat.
Tried lotions and potions
Can't control my emotions.
Now it's me, who's offered a seat.

I watch documentaries.
(Yes, I said documentaries)!
Oh Lord, whatever next?

Can't work this new iPhone.
What even is a "drone"?
And you should see the size of my Text.

I know what you're thinking.
My attitude's stinking.
And I should give myself a break.
Be gentle and kinder.
Now I'm older and wiser.
But SHUT-UP AND PASS ME THAT CAKE.

This menopause issue's a bugger,
I'm telling you.
Nothing will be as it was.
But one thing's for sure
I'm not playing, no more.
I WILL conquer this men-o-pause.

I'm not in denial, this isn't a trial.
The traumas of this change of life.
My symptoms are endless, as God is my witness.
Damn, these tribulations are rife.

I'm determined to beat this.
So, everyone, hear this.
(My side boob just won't play along).
I'll get out of these joggies.
No more with these sloppies.
Sweatshirts and flip flops, be gone.

I'll buy a full swimsuit
And a size-bigger jeans.
I'll embrace these new curves I've got, too.
At the end of the day,
I'm still sexy as hell.
So, menopause, really...
F*&K YOU!

17 April 2021

2 YOU DESERVE IT

Keep moving in the right direction.
Don't get stuck in your past with regret and deflection.
Looking back with melancholy memories.
Days ahead coming are gonna be the best yet.
Stay on your path, it was never gonna be easy.
Want something bad enough
Gotta breathe it in and believe it.
Write a vision on the board and see it through.
Believe in the goodness on its way to you.
Is a done deal, sign here, it's coming true.
Whatever you're dreaming, dream in technicolour.
Put your dream coat on and close your eyes.
Pull back the curtain and reveal your best life.
Live every moment like you're winning.
Put those hot pants on, cos now you're spinning.
Dancing on the stage of your life.
And you're the star.
Don't stop fighting and always be who YOU are.
Everyone is different and that's ok.
So stand up tall and grab the mic
But it's no karaoke.

This is the real deal, wheel of fortune-cookies spinning around.
With slogans manifesting everything
Just turn that frown upside-down.
Cos you got this.
This life story, love glory, battle-winning, victory is yours.
And this is the big one.
The change-your-life, 6 zeros in your bank account one.
And all you have to do to win it is believe it.
So say it with me now and say it loud...
I deserve it.
I DESERVE IT.
Yes, I deserve it.
So, keep on moving don't you stop.
You're going so high, your ears might pop.
Be the best that you can be and leave the rest.
The doubters and the nay-sayers in the rear view.
The ones who you need, will find YOU!
Surround yourself with humble, loving, truth.
And your people will be there to raise the roof
And celebrate YOU.

So be grateful for all you got.
Not everyone's gonna like you – and so what?
Work hard for the good ones, let the rest go.
Friends are like seasons, they'll come and go.
Just keep moving in the right direction. Play the movie of your life with scene selection.
And remember there's always the option of a different ending.
Nothing's ever final, move the goal posts and take the challenge
Life's not a penalty shoot-out with no goalie
Where's the fun in that?
Bater up, on the plate – but no bat?
Not you, you're on your own path.
Home run, Hole-in-one, Formula One, World Cup and Gold Medals adorn your neck.
Meditate and reflect.
And always believe what's next is bigger and better and fuller and fatter.

And you deserve it.
You deserve it.
Yes. You really do deserve it.

28 Aug 2021

3 A DAUGHTERS' GOODBYE

You wanted me and so I came.
But you weren't quite ready for the game.
His heart now shared because of me.
Taken unawares, were we.
No room for me to be just me.
You tried (I hoped), not to punish me.
Unprepared for such a force.
Our relationship was difficult; terse.
But through it all, we never left.
Too steadfast and not bereft.
Memories of my Family stay.
Happy times of Christmas days, Sunday lunches,
Summer fetes, Girl Guide badges, fancy dress,
Gymnastics, singing, egg & cress!
Values of an age I miss.
Our family always greeted with a kiss.
Cakes were baked, well, just in case.
Don't make a fuss "for goodness' sake"!
Stories of "us" as I grew.
Fond recitals, most with you.
Best foot forward, come on now.
Dad's waiting, I can hear him saying.
"Come on Wendy, time's a wasting"

Holding up your favourite flowers,
A dozen yellow roses.
Our precious memories of those hours.
He always went the extra mile. And always with
that cheeky Bernard smile!
Don't worry Mum, they're all there waiting,
Nana, Grandpa, George and Gertrude.
All the souls you lovingly nurtured.

But now it's time for me to say goodbye.
To my Mum; but how do I?

With an overwhelming sadness, yes.
And a hint of melancholic rage (that we won't
speak again in coming days).
Forgiveness and love, now residing here.
All is quiet, calm my dear.
A complicated love, for some.
A daughters' kiss
Goodbye, to Mum.

01 December 2020

4 BEFORE I LAY MY HEAD TO SLEEP

Before I lay my head to sleep
I wish to thank some of my peeps.
For being there when times were tough.
For chicken soup when I felt rough.
You made me laugh instead of cry.
You made me stop asking "why?"
And turned up when I needed you.
Thank you, thank you, all of you.

Na night x

02 February 2013

5 FORGIVING THE BULLIES

Seems like forgiveness is the key to
Set you free from holding on to
Old resentments, which just hurt you.
When the perpetrators probably don't even
remember who you even are.

Except when they were family,
They probably forgot your angst and laughed it
off while you just choked on their bitter, unkind
broth and dribble.
Served with a smile and a sarcastic quip or two.

Bet they don't remember fully how much they
bullied and hurt you.
But you do.

Their jealousy and hurtful words
Dig deep into your skin which
By now, should be thick.
But the memories, well, they just make you feel
sick.

Your pathetic symptomatic knee-jerk reactions
make you want to take action; even now,

But you know how that will just make you the lesser being.
Stooping to their level of harsh words and wrong- doings
And well, that's not really you.
So, you forgive.
Or at least you try to.

Forget the shit they threw and humiliation reigning,
Dripping of the evil whipping of your personality.
Prosecutions, endless ridiculing, and threats.

A test to your character.
Whether you stood your ground or folded.
Giving in to the lies they told and attacking your self-belief and worth.
Spreading gossip and dirt and laughing in your face as they amuse at your demise and lack of responses returning.
They just see your cheeks are burning and they laugh.
But the harder they were on you.
Still hurts you when you remember who colluded to enslave your life.

In dark thoughts and issues.
Taking the piss!
Who the fuck did they think they we're dealing with?

I wonder where they are now.
And if their troubles look them down?
Revenge is a dish best served cold.
Ha! I bet they look old.

But I forgive, because look at me now.
It's me who is winning.
There's no denying.
Yes, I'm forgiving .
Live and let living.
But never forgetting.

They know what they did.
And karma well, we all know what she'll give.

18 February 2018

6 HOW I LOVE TO TRAVEL

As I travel the world, I
Look up to the sky, I See the moon shining bright,
I Watch the stars twinkling light.
How I love to see the sites.

Same sky, different moon.
I'll be back again real soon.
Rolling hills and stunning landscapes.
Yellowstone Park and Jenny Lake.

Snowy peaks, white water creeks.
Log cabins and tents which leak.
Familiar sites, on movie scenes.
Skies so clear and fields of green.

The familiar freeways of
San Fran, New York, and LA.
How I love to get away.

The neon lights of Hong Kong.
In Istanbul, my favourite song
Is The call to prayer, as
I wonder what it's like in there?

The Blue Mosque first rings out her plea.
Then the Red responds immediately.
Surround-sound romance envelopes me.
As I close my eyes and breathe it in.
Immersed in this diversity.

Another plane, another journey.
Experience is more than money.
The world is out there waiting.
So come on, stop procrastinating.

And next time you leave your office Instilled in
this crazy rat-race.
Make a break from your ball and chain.
Those bricks you mortgaged to the hilt.
Forget the guilt, pack your quilt, get on a plane.

Go for a picnic in the dark, in Central Park.
With Fisher Kings and Bridges of Queens.
Where stars have shone in Broadway lights.
How I love to see the sites.

Another day another chance Shall I trek or shall
I dance?
Maybe Venice, the Taj Mahal?
A backpack or a Masquerade Ball?
Wow, I really want to see them all.

Big game on Safari,
The deserts of Kalahari.
Visit Santa Clause at the North Pole.
Wow, so much to do, before I get old.

The Northern Lights, meet the Eskimos.
Lake Tahoe to The Middle East.
Squaw Valley and Sugar Bowl.
Now, I've skied down every piste.

So many places and loads of new faces.
Where on Earth to go next?
Now I'm exhausted and yearn for the sea. A
simpler life somewhere is waiting for me.

Somewhere with palm trees, warm sand under foot.
A cocktail, a hammock, and a really good book.
The sun on my face and the breeze from the sea.
But this time, I think, I just need to find me.

So, maybe an Ashram in India would do it.
Sell all that I own and just wander the planet.
See the whole world before I die.
See all seven wonders, sail all seven seas.

Maybe I just won't come back. Not much to keep me in London these days.

Now all that is left to do.... is pack!

05 Nov 2017

7 THE COVID POEM

I'm "working from home" today.
At least that's what I'm saying.
In my onesie on the sofa,
Watching Netflix, where I'm staying.
Series after series, stopping only for the loo.
A kitchen break for lentil chips and chocolate biscuits too.
It's days like this, which seem to be becoming normal now.
Wandering where my next pay cheque Is coming from and how?
The news comes on and here we go,
Boris Johnson blah, blah, blah!
Dominic Cummings evil announcements...
"Stay home, save lives", ra ra ra.
Global Pandemic, Covid deaths and horrid stories.
Existence as we know it, changed, all because of the f*&king Tories.

Yes, I'm struggling, and today is one of those days.
When I move from room to room in a depressed, confusing daze.

I don't want to talk or answer the phone.
To speak or to explain.
That today I'm struggling more than they know.
Today, I am in pain.
Can't seem to shake it off.
Facebook posts of people offering a helping hand.
Meaningless to me.
As I'm usually the helper, not the helpless helpee.

The difficulty of reaching out, but with nothing much to say.
How hard it is, for all of us
To leave the house some days.
Why can't I just shake this off?
And how do I explain?

Nothing much to moan about
Just anxious, feeling down.
Some days I just can't face the world.
So, I'll stay here, on the sofa,
Where I'm safe, until I can.

20 January 2021

8 FAKES & REMAKES

Round and round the record goes.
Stay alert and on your toes.
The world keeps turning and
I'm yearning for something genuine and new.
Monkey Magic re-runs on the TV.
Not the Netflix remake, it's vexing me.

Nothing new to turn up.
Round and round, they round up.
All that has come before.
Is being reworked, remade, and churned out.
Just give me something new in this world of
fakes and remakes.
'Cause I'm burned out.

I've got 42 inches of High Definition.
But by definition of the content it spews
It should be renamed "Low and Depressing".
Pressing me to find another way.
Blaring out bloody thunder and misery.
And everything around me is steeped in history.
Time to go, got to get lost.
See the sun and sea for real.
Not just in a Facebook post.

My past is all around me, it's time to break free.
Mix up the vibe get out of this closing-in City.
Political agendas pretending to be "woke" up.
Royal family is falling, pick your crown up.
Queeny's having a job to hold her job down now.
Philip at death's door, Harry's title "HRH" out the door.
And now look, he's got a "proper" job!

Nothing new to turn up.
Round and round, they round up.
All that has come before
Is being reworked, remade, and churned out.
Just give me something new in this world of fakes and remakes.
'Cause I'm burned out.

Brexit; the Winter of our European discontent.
British passports now a flag of contempt.
No more manners, so you push and shove.
Faces masked and hands in gloves.
Anti-bac dispensers on every wall.
Keeping you inside as 5g is installed.
World leaders joining the Muppet clan.
No KKK reports, just Paedo' rings and "Orange" fans.
What a crock of shit to bear.

A right to bear arms?
Yeah, 'cause that's a great idea.

Who's in charge now – leader of the free world?
A robot imposter run by Bill Gates some thought.
Batten down the hatches, here comes the Q-Anon onslaught.

CIA infiltrating our Signal, Messenger, and WhatsApp?
End to end encryption – don't believe that!
Nothing's sacred anymore is it Siri? Siri?
Don't call me that, my name's Alexa, innit.
Turn the lights on Alexa… tell us the truth.
Signal error Wi-Fi's dropped, aluminium hats, quick get on the roof.

Nothing new to turn up.
Round and round, they round up.
All that has come before
Is being reworked, remade, and churned out.
Just give me something new in this world of fakes and remakes.
'Cause I'm burned out.

Netflix, Sky Q, Boob jobs, Housewives of wherever and surgery botches.
The demise of mankind rolling out as the world sits and watches.
Mainstream media spewing their lies.
Judge Rinder, Loose Women, Philip & Holly
Bring back Ab Fab – "Patsy where's the Bolli?"
Not much to celebrate and who wants to drink champagne on your Jack?
Secrets, lies and sexy scandal.
Nothing new to hear, so handle.
Reality TV taken to new levels.
No distinction from the truth and the fiction.

Every day's a pay day hold your hand out. Your piece of demon flesh is being dolled out.
30 pieces of silver in a cash for gold envelope.
Medicine for all is growing – finally, hey man, that's dope.

Nothing new to turn up.
Round and round, they round up.
All that has come before
Is being reworked, remade, and churned out.
Just give me something new in this world of
fakes and remakes.
'Cause I'm burned out.

Black Lives Matter and we know that.
Not sure whether to take a knee or to stand up.
Oprah and Meghan versus the crown.
Piers Morgan's big storm out and dress down.
Meanwhile where's Prince Andrew?
He's gone underground!
Epstein mean-machine, kiddy-fiddling,
hide-and-seek.
What a bunch of back-stabbing hypocrites.
Ugly, rotten, human misfits.
All the best artists dead and gone.
But at least their music lives on.

No concerts or live shows to remember.
No memories to share with fan club members.
And friends too far away to lend their shoulders
for us to cry on.
No flights or respite.
No holidays and now fines to pay.
With what? The money we haven't earned.
From the lockdown, as our businesses are all
shut down and up turned.
Our fingers burned by the Tory government.
Here we go again, but there's no competition.
What we need is a revolution.
Yes, what we need is a REVOLUTION.

That's not a revelation though is it?

We need a new beginning, like a re-set.
Or is that what they're planning – is that what
this is?

It's a worldwide re-set - check your mindset.
And your standing.
Are the aliens planning on their landing?
I'd like to think so, that would be so cool.
But we'd probably destroy them all too.

Nothing new to turn up.
Round and round, they round up.
All that has come before
Is being reworked, remade, and churned out.
Just give me something new in this world of fakes and remakes.
'Cause I'm burned out.

Stop this nonsense, please.
I've had enough!

14 March 2021

9 THE MAP OF MY LIFE

Half a century I've walked this earth.
A long road travelled with twists and turns and mirth.
Tears of joy and cries of pain along the way.
But I dust myself off and get back up again and again.
Worn so many pairs of shoes out.
But my soul remains whole.
I will spread my wings and fly away.
But I always come back to myself.
No more doormat, foot-wiping, face-slapping imposters.
These intruders can't stop my enthusiasm.

I'll keep moving and driving onwards and upwards.
Making the most of the cul-de-sacs and dead ends.
Rolling into the tight corners and speeding out of the bends.
I've got the wanderlust and I'm never scared.
Adventures are waiting, so search and find and share.

Not sure quite which way I'll go.
But life's for the living, so come with me, let's go!
Hold my hand and let's jump.
Don't hold me back, come on, let's jump.
It's gonna be the next great adventure of my life.

Who knows, maybe I'll meet my soulmate, maybe
even become a wife!
Nothing ventured, nothing gained.
Where in the world will this all take place?
A beachy paradise would be nice.
With some sunshine on my face.

An easy life with friends around me.
Someone beautiful to share and laugh with me.
I'll get the maps and search the universe.
Check my friends and neighbours' favourite
places.
Ignore the doubt written all over their faces.
'Cause I'm not scared.
Never have been.
And all in my search to find "him".
I'll check my route and grab my compass.

Or maybe, I just need a final destination.
The only way is up.
Now, where did I put that sat nav?

29 May 2018

10 EVERYONE IS BORN BEAUTIFUL

Everyone is born beautiful.
Perfection is the key.
Perfect for their mission in this life.
Exactly how they are meant to be.

It's trauma and hatred which grows.
Changing our perspectives.
Nature versus nurture shows.
Our parents' retrospectives.

Shape us, how we view and act
Molding our existence.
Teaching us their history facts.
Sometimes forcing their persistence.

If all of us would look inside.
And listen to our hearts.
Be gentle with opinions, kind.
It would be a better start.

Take away the jealousy
The bitter and the hurt
Meditate and slow the pace
Alleviate all things terse.

Everyone is perfect.
Until we're told we're not.
Then negativity reflects.
How amazing if this stopped?

Damage begats damage, so
Be kind and gentle now
Live with love and off you go
Teach your offspring how.

Children are born perfect.
Their path is up to you.
Teach them modesty, respect,
Honour and of course, forgiveness too.

I leave you now with words of love.
A request that you take head.
For the ones you teach, who rise above.
Will be the ones who'll lead.

6 April 2021

11 FRONTLINE WARRIOR

I'm a soldier.
No sit down, stand back, keep quiet, push over.
I'm a Frontline Warrior.

I'm a say what I feel until I see you understand kind of gal.
And if you reel, that's ok. It's just not your day.

I'm a go-getter.
I'm a place your bets kind o' Jet-stream racing driver.
Foot down, hold tight 0-60 in a hot minute.
And I bring it and I give it.
All. Day. Long.

And I won't stop until I'm done.
Can't keep up – so now you gotta run.
I'm pushing through, and if I'm with you, you better hold tight.
Cos I'm going into battle and we're gonna win this fight.

I've got the scars to prove it and the stripes.
I'm a General in the Army of Life.
No fight too small to march to Victory.
So, are you with me?
Cause if you are, you need to know this...
I'm a Frontline Warrior.
And we've got this.

9 August 2021

12 THANK YOU JULIA

For listening, sometimes, even though you're busy.
For being Irish, gorgeous, blonde, and dizzy.
for supporting me, even when I'm wrong.
For every bloody annoying song!
For being the greatest Mum I know.
For knowing all the things you know.
For hanging in there; you're never lazy.
For laughing every time I said "Moy Neime's Ian Paisley".
For being KIND and letting people off scot-free.
For allowing me, to just be me.
For loving me anyway, every day.
For your generosity when I came to stay.
For being so brilliant and bloomin' clever.
Just remember that I will never
Take for granted what you give.

And I hope we'll be friends for as long as we live.
So, I write this poem for you today.

Because I won't be there for your special birthday.
I know your day will be filled with magic.
And that your hangover will then be tragic!

So darling, have a most wonderful Birthday.
I'd give anything to be by your side today.
One more thing before I say "toodle-oo".
Thank you, Julia... for just being you.

02 October 2015

13 TO JULIA

Hi darling. How are you my lovely friend?
Gosh I miss you my dear.
I see your face every day.
Full of love and laughter on my mantlepiece.
A printed reminder I will always keep.
I remember the friendship and the love for one
another, which we built.
It will always be my stalwart ember.
Never leaving my gripping hand.
The joy you found in the simplest of things.
A fresh face full of wonderful you.
A smile to take most every pain away.
Knowing you were there, and my friend.
It's so long since we just sat in silence.
(As if that's something we could ever do!)
Memories wrapped in bonds which never tire.
Drunken giggles, dancing madness.
Your echo still is ringing here.
It is my treasured gift to keep.
My trinket of those days we relished.
'Til we meet and drink and laugh and dance again.
I will forever cherish and hold it tight and sip, not
gulp for fear it might just disappear.

But never forget I'm here for you.
Though I'm over here and you are there.
Sometimes it feels so very far.
Just reach out - I'll be right there; remember this
and never fear.
I love you my friend and miss you more.
Don't you ever shed a tear.

You are a wonderful, silly, clever, amazing girl.
And I love you to the moon and stars and around
the world.

3 September 2020

14 TO ANNALISA

Her perfectly plumped and defined lips are the colour of every scratch she's earned.

She will adorn your skin with a little piece of her soul every time she etches on yours.

With every needle, the devil's in the detail and she pains at perfection, striving for a flawless view.

Not just for her, but to please you too.

She tickles the edge of a life less ordinary.

No serpents allowed in her garden you know, just a friendly snake ascending her ladder, called Dino.

A sign she's not to be messed with.

Isn't that right, Mistress?

No distress here as her comforter Kujo, a trusty Staffordshire Terrier is always next to her.

Her rescued companion returns the favour within his daily loyalty rituals.

And she adores him.

Annalisa: A woman with a heart of gold.

Sweet as sugar and bitter as spice, but never unkind to the pallet.

Deeper waters run deeper still.

Like many a discarded ocean fling, she'll rise again, with stronger will.

Striding forth with warrior veins, not afraid to tread on lines and watch her reign.

She'll cross boundaries to stretch her enemies or allow a master to rule her push her and challenge her, never losing sight of her minds' eye.

Or is it a dream?

She will always be a Queen.

Her gang is here, but the streets don't ring with bullets yonder.

At all hours of the night, you'll see her wander.

Her armory of gentle sharps ensures all her princes adorn her colours.

Even if they're only black and white

There are always 300 shades of grey.

The accent of an Italian father, but with the beauty of Madonna's mother

She smiles and melts a thousand ice caps

Perfectly polished white and gleaming

Like uniformed officers ready and wielding.

Her soldiers are ready to die for her.

She parts the blood sea of possibility, seemingly inviting.

But which offering today: challenge or mercy?

You'll find out.

Respectfully gentle with a sweetness not quite uncovered.

Like the tip of a treasure barely buried waiting to be discovered.

When she lights up it's an inviting, delightful exhibition.

A gentle display of what's gone but what has stayed with her, is worth the waiting.

So, if you see her, be kind, be gentle.

Or she may bite you with a sting that you'll remember forever.

But you can bet she'll kiss you better.

Never harming until you push her.

Annalisa, she has a body for sin, but don't be tempted.

Unlock her mind and she'll be YOUR temptress, forgiving, playful but relentless.

Annalisa, amore mio.
Ti Amo.

12 September 2020

15 THE ROMANIAN PRINCE

First you see the designer shades, the curls, and that shining pout.

When he smiles, he's awkward and slightly shy, but spears you with his arrogant defence.

One blow with an extension of kindness, his shield drops like budgie smugglers at a rave.

Autistically artistic; he's fantastic.
He has no clue of his loveliness; although he'd have you think completely the opposite.

Attitude a pre-requisite in his designer-covered façade, which conceals an introverted genius, crying out for acceptance and deliverance. Someone to love him in his completeness.

Slightly more acceptable than Edward, his scissor hands are way more creative than the confines of an undeserving salon.

Painting his quirkiness, drawing nurture from sources he doesn't know how to fully tap into just yet.

He is kind and keenly helpful, but is easily hurt and his responses are overly evil, which little does he realise, shows a sensitivity to his protagonists.

This child-like boyish charmer, like a Prince with slightly dented armour, is misunderstood and delightfully churlish in his loveliness.

Comic charactures capture and enrapture his attention, leading him away from reality, to a world where it's easier for him to comprehend.

But he's real to me. And he's lovely. (When he's not angry and evil and switchy!)

The Romanian Prince!

15 September 2020

16 TO SIMONE

So, cousin Sim, you're leaving us!
But you'll never be alone.
Don't fret pet, we'll keep an eye,
On all things Harrow Road!

We'll be here, just cracking on.
As you make your merry way.
Hopefully we'll all come down
For a cheeky Margate getaway.

The boys will miss you, that's for sure.
Those scallies, what make your crew.
Denver, Clappers, Ali, Atlas
Chemist and me, too!

We'll miss you cuz it's plain to see.
Life just won't be the same.
Without our Harrow Road harlot
It really is a shame.

But off to pastures new you'll trek.
With old adventures to have, ahead.
Don't hold back or give a damn.
Time to go get your Larry lamb.

May Juicy Lucy's Balls be with you!
Giving you the drive.
We all love you cousin Sim.
So, it's "adios", but not goodbye!

We wish you joy and happiness.
We're really gonna miss you.
Safe journey Sim my friend.
May fun and laughter always follow you.

30 July 2019

17 MARRIED 12, TOGETHER 17

A celebration of love and laughter.

Lovers and best friends, you're truly a team.
Married for Twelve, together Seventeen.
With family and friends, who stood to bear witness.
It's your wedding day, we are honouring with this.

On this day you swore to have and to hold.
Nothing seemed out of your reach, or too bold.
A day full of promises, foundations were laid.
The love built here, will always, ALWAYS prevail.

Something old, something new, something borrowed and something blue.
The dress, the occasion, the flowers, the veil;
Adorning the Princess, as she walked down the aisle.

Fairy-tale moments, forever etched in your souls.
Shared dreams and ambitions of your "together life goals".
Remember each day that you made your commitment.
To "love and to cherish"; the sexiest statement.

*"Love is patient and kind it does not envy or boast.
It is not arrogant or rude, it does not judge or
resent. Love bears ALL things.
Believes ALL things, hopes ALL things and LOVE
endures ALL things."*

It's not always going to be romance and roses.
But Adam & Chan it was each other you chose.
A reminder today of your Love Story plot.
(Just in case for a minute there, you might have
forgot).

SEVENTEEN years, and I'm here to remind you.
That your love is a DEEP love.
A love that is true.

Your love WILL sustain.
It WILL always endure.
Of course, there'll be times when you won't feel
so sure.

So briefly reflect on each solemn vow.
It will bring you right back to the here and the now.
Write love letters and keep the romance alive.
Be thoughtful and generous but most of all, kind.

Hold each other and appreciate how far you've journeyed together.
There is NO storm out there
You two cannot weather.

Your lives are entwined
May NO man put asunder.
Because you two are a team.
Full of life, love, and wonder.

29 August 2021

18 BATTLE SCARS – TO EMILY

Bonded by our battle scars.
Different stories, different wars.
A life of tears, our rivers cried.
Still wielding our respective sythes.

Hiding our pain, we wear our masks.
Sipping comfort from life's hip flask.
We recognised the fights we fought.
Some lessons learned; some lessons taught.

Knocked to the ground; used, abused.
Both our spirits and our egos bruised.
But we stood up each and every time.
Hiding our pain behind our smiles.

Life and soul? If they only knew.
What troubles we've had to go through.
No day to end with stifled breath.
A life of grief and waters shed.

Our childless lives, we seem untouched.
A future lost, we left unclutched.
It never leaves it won't depart.
Loneliness lingers inside our hearts.

Unlikely friends, that knowing look.
A glance that someone else mistook.
We won't be judged; they just don't know.
The lengths to which we had to go.

So, hold your head up, grab my hand.
I got you girl. I understand.
We will prevail these darkest days.
The fog will lift, as will the haze.

Some friends we lost along the way.
Left holes for ever and a day.
Their souls will never fly away.
And guide us each and every day.

Salute your strength and thank the stars.
We've survived, with ALL our battle scars.

06 May 2021

19 THE FAST LAYNE EXPERIENCE

With skin so smooth, like fine Godiva.
That look he gives, of molten lava.
Those eyes which sparkle with playful twinkle
The crease above his lip, which crinkles.
His boyish humour and love of life.
Melts away the deepest strife. Infectious humour
drips and settles.
Perfect moments – just got better.
A mouth you long to linger longer.
His touch; deftly agile, strong, yet tender.
Are you ready, cos he's gonna send ya?
Round the bend, then come back and get ya.
His laugh, delights with unique reverb.
Histrionics hidden in his truths and proverbs.
Gentle, kind, and full of life.

Warning:

Can't be tamed, observe only in the wild.
Free, unchained and he'll return.
Don't be tempted – fingers burned.
Lessons will be learned, so let him go.
Round and round the world he goes.

A gentleman for sure, a scholar.
Always wants to please another.
Life has filled his playbook copy.
But you'll never see him sad or stroppy.
Redman; a species unto himself.
You'll know you've met him, but not until
He's left and now you're all a quiver.
Get in your Layne, he'll brush and whisper.

Don't take over, lean into the bend.
Feel the wind in your hair and blend.
If he were food, he'd be the taster menu.
One dessert to share, two spoons.

Seemingly romantic moments
Second nature, first class treatment.
His eclectic taste buds know no bounds.
But always with feet on solid ground.
He dines with gusto at the table of life.
He'll cull your Oyster with his shucking knife.
No recipe too fine or simple.
It's all an exquisite surprise to this one.

If he were a yacht, he'd be a Lazzara Sport
But no docking or mooring in the port.
He'd be out there on the ocean, free.
Sipping rum on deck, with tunes and breeze.

Always surrounded by an air of mystery.
This AMG, M3, Carrera Sport Pack luxury.
Like Pinin Ferrina with nubuck leather interior.
Custom, first class Louis Vuitton backpack,
Label warrior.

Always on the lookout and opportunity always
knocks.
Right place, right time, like Patek Philipp, but on
3 different clocks.
GMT or Middle East or is it Caribbean time?
Forget that - he's on his own grind.

An ageless old soul, RnB, Jazz Funk and Motown
groover.
He'll give you the best night, he's a shaker and
a smooth mover.

A survivor and a trooper;
Sky diving, rock climbing Dare-devil "try anything once" kinda geezer.
With the enthusiasm of an excited teenager.
That's why he has to keep on moving.
Fingers in all sorts of pies, as long as they're Vegan.
Live fast, die young – not his style; his body is his temple.
And your alter is the one he'll worship, treasure and respect.
Until the next one.
And there will be a next one, do you remember the warning?

"Can't be tamed, observe only in the wild
Free, unchained and he'll return Don't be tempted – fingers burned".

Don't forget now.
Stay in your Layne.
And avoid that unnecessary world of pain.

'Cause he's the player of HIS game.
He's the Blackjack, with a full deck, stacked in his favour.
The Ace of Spades and the King of Clubs make 21!
Take the hand he's dealing and stick. How many cards in a pack?
That's like asking him his age.
Don't gamble with his years of experience, you'll waiver.
Lick the lollipop he's giving you for now and savour.

Laughter is his medicine.
(That and Maca and Moringa Seeds).
Young at heart, he'll be in yours forever.
Once sipped and tasted, his essence lingers.
Yes, life in the fast Layne is not to be missed.
So, share him with pleasure, or fade the memory of that kiss.
Just go with it, the ecstasy and sweet release.

Hold tight, you've just had the Fast Layne Experience.

5 August 2021

20 TO DOMINIQUE

Where do I start with a woman like you?
A force to be reckoned with.
That's certainly true!

A brood full of talent, your kids do you proud.
A voice full of authority. No need to be loud.

Look at you now, Fifty years on this earth.
Surrounded by us lot, to show you, your worth.

We'd like to say thank you Dom, for all that you've
done.
For the parties you've hosted, to all the birthdays
you've come.

For showing us how to move forward in life.
For just getting on with your "troubles and strifes".

For not giving up when we all needed a leader.
For being there smiling, you couldn't be sweeter.

For being our beacon when times got a bit tough.
For having our backs through the smooth and
the rough.

Now there's a few things we still need to cover.
Like the fact that you're a brilliant Mother.

Kids growing up now, your 2 Border Collies.
Your determination and grit handling life's various
follies!

All dealt with by you, with an air and a grace.
Steadfast and loyal with a smile on your face.

Max tall and handsome, now at Uni - so cool.
Evelyn's sixteen now and nobody's fool.

Cecelia's a teenager – and just like her Dad.
All their adventures in life, still to have.

Beaded with silver, but inside you're gold.
No one would believe you're Fifty years old.

Still funky and sassy and down with the kids.
Generous, tenacious – qualities with no lid.

Funny, sarcastic, and great fun to boot. Always
up for a cocktail – Dominique, you're a hoot.

Fifty is the new thirty, take it from me. We just sit down a bit more (and no more climbing trees)!

But tonight is your night, to party and dance. And we want you to know how special you are to us.

So Happy Birthday Dominique, you're our Diamond for sure.
The matriarch of this mad family; we couldn't love you more.

Don't worry honey, there's loads more to come. We're your supporters forever, love from the parts of your sum!

19 May 2021

21 THE ART OF STANDING

A multi-layered, creative soul.
With depth and love inside.
A gentle man who doesn't know.
The beauty of his kind.

A friend, whose laugh is everything.
Our memories I will treasure.
The nights we giggle, dance and sing.
The Art of Standing is your pleasure.

African roots adorn his work.
Colourful, layered, and bold.
Emotion expressed by splatters and quirks.
Now he's Royal Academy Gold.

From Zimbabwe to the Maldives.
From London and Russia, with love.
He's open to every opportunity.
And each placement fits like a glove.

Marc Standing, he's not just an Artist.
He's my friend, who'll stand the test.
The Art of Standing is simply magnificent.
And to me, he'll always be the best.

19 September 2021

22 MAID MARION, THE MIGHTY

She's a Rockstar!
It's simple.
That's what springs to mind when you see her.
And you secretly probably want to be a bit like her.

This woman exudes class in each and every stride.
Just to be her friend will fill you with pride.
5 kids, 2 husbands she's the Queen we admire.
To walk by her side, is to simply rise higher.

Expensive and elegant, cool, funky and chic.
This woman will always be at her peak.
A life of cool stories that you'll all want to hear.

Maid Marion, The Mighty.
I'm so happy you're here.

24 July 2022

23 GOODBYE RYA

To my beloved Westie, 11-05-2006 to 21-12-21

You walked beside me, looking up.
You made me laugh and cry.
Your memory will long remain
In every rainbow in the sky.

From the very first encounter
We were bonded at the start.
Your paw prints and your little bark
Will stay locked inside my heart.

I knew this fateful day would come.
And when it did, I knew.
To take you over that rainbow bridge.
While I was holding and kissing you.

You were fiercely loved by everyone.
Full of Westitude and fun.
You were my loyalest companion.
My heart's broken, now our time together's done.

I'll miss you, "Rya, Monkey Mya".
My feisty Westie bear.
Don't you fret, I won't forget.
I'll see you in every memory we shared.

Don't worry little Rya, I will be ok.
Knowing you are resting now.
Is how I'll get through these days.

You were my little soldier.
A trooper to the end.
I'll love you always and forever.
My beautiful best friend.

21 December 2021

24 HAPPY BIRTHDAY TT

I met him "out out" – I think we were clubbing.
Back in the day – when I was right gobby.
You could hear his laugh across the dance floor.
I knew then he was a decent bloke, for sure.
He's big and he's strong, is our Tony.
But really, he's just a big softy.
The Macho-ist man and we know it.
But he just wants to be loved – so don't blow it.
He fixes our cars when they're broken.
So, look after him proper – not just a token.
If, like me, you drive like a c*nt – he's your man.
Whether it's a Fiat, a Jag, or a getaway Van!
A diamond for sure and we love our TT.
You're just a big Teddy.
Happy Birthday sweetie.

14 September 2021

25 THE CHARLIE NEXTDOOR

About four years ago I moved in, to this street.
Primarily, to get myself back on my feet.
I went into the garden
And said "I beg your pardon?"
There was a woman stood there
With long chocolate brown hair
She was smiling a lot
She said "Hello, I'm Charlotte
I live here and this is my son".
She said "How exciting, and Welcome".
Now four years on, I am glad to extend
That she's not just my neighbour, she's also my friend.
We've had some adventures, got drunk and talked nonsense.
We've passed bottles of wine and cigarettes through the fence.
She's always happy to do you a favour.
She's lovely, is Charlotte, my friend and my neighbour.
She's an actress you know.
I've been to her shows.
She's talented, clever and really quite funny.

And she likes a glass of Rosé (or 2), when it's sunny.
I'm lucky that when I moved into this street.
Primarily, to help me get back on my feet.
We've supported each other through some difficult times.
Although one birthday she nearly poisoned me with limes.
Even if we move away, our friendship won't waiver.
She's lovely, is Charlotte; my friend and my neighbour.
For those of you here, who know Charlotte as well.
You all know that lately she's been through some hell.
But now she's on track and she's got her smile back.
Darling we all love you, you are a class act.
We're all lucky to have met you, that is a fact.
Charlotte we're all here for you today.
To wish you a very, VERY happy Birthday.

9 September 2014

26 I WEAR RED

I wear red, so you don't see me bleed.
When my mascara runs in the rain, it's not real.

When my soul is so trodden
I'm like an old pair of shoes.
Which cannot be fixed with just any old glue.

But watch me rise from the ashes.
I am Phoenix.
Listen to my words, can you hear this?

Sometimes I don't know how to stop the seething, crying and reeling.
So yeah, I'm wearing red, so you can't see the blood.
From the broken hearts of past years and the misery of all those scars and tears.

You trod on me like I'm a puddle of mud.
How are you going to stop it seeping?
Now you made it start.
It's not stopping.
But I'm hoping.
I need to believe you will turn it in.
Bring me back from the brink.

Keep me afloat.
Don't let our love sink.
Drowning in my anxiety.
Whilst watching you drip with apathy.

So disappointing, but now I wear a shield.
No more easy knee-drop yield.

Yes, I wear red, so you can't see me bleed.
But the stain of heartbreak and beatings is darker
than you could ever see.

09 August 2018

27 THAT SECTION
OF NIGHT

When your head is too heavy with the weight of your thoughts.

With the rattle of insecurities and the "what if's", which taunt.

When you're lying there, waiting for sleep to brush by.

And you lay, wide awake, but you still close your eyes.

You can hear the cogs turning, the possibilities, the yearning.

The silence of no-one, to just hold you close.

The bottom of the bed empty, where once you wrapped toes.

All this goes on in that section of night.

When you've turned out the light.

It's now 3am and you went to bed at midnight.

The man in the moon, shines right through the window.

And you can't get the images of that last Facebook video to stop playing in slowmo.

So much so now, you must put on the light.
To reassure you and centre, to ease down the frights.

The "maybe I should do that"?
And "I definitely mights". The "To Do" list, you lay there and mentally write.

All this goes on in that section of night.
When you've turned out the light. It's now 3am and you went to bed at midnight.

Check the world clock on your iPhone.
Just to see who might be online.
Friends in LA, Hanoi, or Dubai.
Maybe send a quick WhatsApp to say "Hi."
Then realise you're too tired to engage or reply.
But not sleepy enough either, to lay back down and try.

Oh good, here it comes the "I've had enough" yawn!
Hope I'll be asleep soon, before the light of the dawn.

Because all this goes on in that section of night.
When you've turned out the light.
It's now 3am and you went to bed at midnight.

So Good night. Sleep tight.

16 April 2018
(3.23am)

28 THE MONEY MANIFESTATION SONG

Dollars, Euros, Pounds and Pence.
Dirhams, Yen and Lira.
Even if it's just one pence.
I can feel it getting nearer.

Money for my house, my car, my lifestyle and
my dogs.
Money's raining down on me.
Now I have my dream job.

Working for myself creates abundance all around.
Living a life of love and health.
My income knows no bounds.

Stephanie Houghton's GLOBAL brand.
Bringing in ten trillion RAND.
Travels far and wide we go
Watch my manifesting flow.

Feel DELICIOUS energy.
Bring the Dollars back to me.
Sports car in the drive, I love.
Maserati - fits like glove.

Money, money, everywhere.
In the Bank, under the stairs.
Money, money everywhere.
So much and I love to share.

My home La Bella Casa Blanca.
Really feeds my soul.
Designed it, built it - every brick.
It truly was my goal.

Sunshine on the deck today.
Ocean Crystal Blue.
Loving partner kisses me.
With love that's deep and true.

La Bella Casa Blanca.
My Poetry Books and my Car.
I'm ready for it Universe.
Come on and raise the bar.

People come from far and wide.
I'm full of love and burst with pride.
Money, money everywhere.
So much and I love to share.

Meditate and feel the vibe
We're in the "5 Percenters" Tribe.
Forbes list writers now are waiting.
Can you feel it - I'm vibrating.

Thank you, Universe for this.
I'm leaning in, to feel my BLISS.
Trust the process, now surrender.
I've got the funds to be a BIG spender!

14 April 2019

29 YOUR MOTHER MADNESS

While you sleep.
As you lay there, I ponder.
I take the day off my face,
Contemplate and wander through the twists and
turns of our day.
Today wasn't a great day.
But it was made better with your voice at the end
of the phone.
Didn't want to drone on about my bad mood,
But you did.
Patiently listening to my tears as I flipped my lid.
No rhyme nor reason, just a rubbish day.
And can't take any teasing when I feel this way.
And you know this.
You're patient and kind
As you
Listen to me unwind and calm down.
Iron out my frown with a simple kiss.
Blood pressure easing.
Voice pitch not quite as piercing, and I calm
down.

We do the same for each other.
Earlier this week it was your turn.
Tried again with her and your fingers got burned.
As she turned against you again.
Mums do that, I've learned.
Mine is the same on occasion.
Much less now though, with dementia.
But I still hear her words that tormented.
Still, we recognise a resilience in one another.
A bitterness towards a rubbish brother;
Yep, I know that score.
The playing field which never levels to your favour.
Still the pain lessens more.
With each barrier we form.
Now too high for them to climb over.
But somehow still able to penetrate.
Feeling disappointment and hate,
Is hate too strong a word?
'Cos in the moment I know we feel it.
Darker thoughts with every disagreement.
We want them to be ok for selfish reasons.
So that they might actually be nice to us with a
reassuring consistency, but they insist on being
mean.

It's their default.
Not our fault.
But we endure the challenge.
Believing in respite.
Despite everything they show us.
They really just don't know us.
Not really.
Cos if they did, why would they make us feel like this?
Alone and sad and dis... disappointed disrespected, disowned, disregarded dis dis dis!
But here you are, in my bed, sleeping.
Comforting to know I'll be in your arms presently and hopefully dreaming pleasantries.
If only I could sleep!
So, I get up and write.
No counting sheep.
Just a note to let you know we're gonna be ok.
Never mind the Mother Madness.
We're good.
We survived it thus far.
Can't touch us here, at least.
So, we're gonna be fine.

No, we are fine. We're great.
Rant now expelled on the laptop keyboard, I stop.
Under the covers, sleep now descends and calm.
Night night.
See you in the morning light when everything will seem better.
Wrapped in each other's shelter.

09 March 2019

30 THE BIG TRANSITION

What do you say when someone tells you they're now a "he", or a "she", when all you've known them as, was what they were before?

Do you say, "Well done mate", or" nice one babe"?

What's the appropriate way for them to tell you? "I'm not them anymore, I'm Trans"?

They've transitioned, so everything you thought about them is now switched up, changed around and how do I not mess up by calling you "he" or "she" or "them" or "they"?

Who fucking cares?

"They", no matter whether they are "he" or "she" or "them" or "they" - "they" will always be the person you love.

Only now they might just see what you see and love themselves a little bit more now too.

You see it's not about you, it's about "them" or "they" or "him" or "her".

Not a conversation to deter you from your friendship or relationship or whatever "they" are to you, "they" still are.

They're just a better version of themselves, because now they feel real.

For the first time in their life, they see themselves in the mirror and don't wonder who the fuck they're looking at.

Instead of seeing an imposter or a fake, now they're the real deal and they feel like themselves. At last.

How would you know what that feels like unless you've been there?

You wouldn't; there aren't words to explain other than this:

How would you feel if you had to wear a dress and be girl but all you wanted to do was

climb the trees just like the other boys.

Play with dolls and not their toys?

You don't know, 'cos you can't possibly know how that feels.

And I'm not talking about "tom-boy syndrome" here.

What does "Trans" even mean to you and me?
Again... who fucking cares?
Because it's not about us.
It's about "them" or "they" or "he" or "she" or "him" or "her".
And we love them no matter what.
Don't we?

And if you're struggling with their transition, imagine how they've been feeling; trapped in the wrong body for eternity.
Oh yeah that's right.
You can't possibly understand. Can you?

So, when they come out and tell you "Hey, I'm not "her" or "him" or "them" anymore but I'm ME and look at ME, aren't I great?"
If it's not, and YOU don't feel the same, well that's on you.
The only response should be.
I love YOU anyway.
And now, hopefully you do too.

06 August 2020

31 THIS TOO SHALL PASS

When the clouds come.
Even when the Sun is out.
When the world just doesn't fit.
And your face is not the one you're looking at in
the mirror.
These are the days you need to stop and sit.
As this too, shall pass.

When the light at the end of your tunnel dims.
And the simple things seem hard to do. When
the kettle never seems to boil and you're on the
outside looking in.
This too, shall pass.

Take a break and rest yourself.
Take some time for you.
Put your feet up, close your eyes.
Just take care of you.
This too, my friend, shall pass.

Even the brightest stars get dark.
So, shine your light on them.
For the ones that need it most are often just forgotten.
The battery might just need changing.
But this too, of course, will pass.

13 May 2020

32 SOMETIMES, I JUST FEEL REALLY SAD

Sometimes, I just feel really sad.
But I don't want to be one of those people you avoid.
I don't want to cry any more.
I don't want to be sad and alone.
And I don't want to be one of those people who just moans.

But sometimes I just feel really sad.
When I'm on my own.
I've had love before, but I let it go.
Now it feels like I'll never find it again.
Maybe that's why my heart is in pain.
I know I have friends, but they'll never know.
How much sometimes I just want to let go.

I stay out, just so I don't have to come home.
I can't stand the noise of the silence.
When I'm on my knees and begging the universe to please.
Let someone find me, before it's too late.
Before I write my epitaph, 'cause I really can't wait.
The emptiness inside just gets fuller.
It consumes me and I can't take it.

I don't want to be sad anymore, I'm dying inside.
I'm desperate to belong and yet just need the end.
I'm not sick, I'm just tired of the fight for my life.
The false smiles and the brave face I wear.
Gets harder and harder to make-up as the lipstick fades.
From the air kisses and the whole charade.
Curtains up let's go again – a new day.
A fight, in pain, constant rain and sadness reigns.
I'm really sad... I just can't explain.
But sometimes, I just feel really sad.

8 June 2014

33 DARK DAYS

When days are dark and gloom engulfs to sour
your taste, you wince.
And all that looms seems treacherous.
All actions feel like waste and since.

When sun is high, but mood is low.
And shadows start closing in on you.
When nothing helps, all news is bad.
All woes surpasses both old and new.

How d'you change and switch it up?
How d'you stop the fear and shame?
As this time around self-pity may win,
No rules or choices in this game.

Do you fold and pass or carry on?
Do you stand firm, strong and tall?
For giving in might kill you yet.
And surely you don't want to fall.

Will you reclaim your winning streak?
Only you can turn it around.
Be the change you want to see
Bring it back and close the deal.

Life is hard, so suck it up.
You're the leader not the sheep.
Rid the monkey on your back.
Take your Aces, Kings and Queens.
For failure here, means JACK.

23 February 2021

34 I WOKE UP SMILING

When I woke up this morning, I was smiling!
Remembering the night before; I'm reeling.
Fingers down my body, was I dreaming?
Feeling so sexy, but was I teasing you boy?
Got me running back for more.
Like I wanna be your toy.
We're gonna take it nice and slow.
And this it how it goes.

When I woke up this morning I was smiling.
Hands down my pjs, was I dreaming? Feeling hot
under the collar, we were writhing and steaming.
Telly me baby, am I dreaming?

Yeah we started off slow and then we steamed in.
Discovering our passion, it was rising.
Shortening of breath, there's no disguising it boy.
Stroking your body, 'til you shiver with joy.

Baby I'm a giver, just wanna please ya.
And next time I come over, gonna show ya.
Grinding and kissing.
It's what I've been missing.
Lover man, tell me was it good too, when I was
touching you?

Taking it slow, just wanna kiss ya.
Roll that tongue where ya wanna, put it on me.
Cos I'm twisting,
Moving my body so you can work it.
Covering every curve you got me winding.
Press up on me yeah, cos now we're grinding.
And I don't mind, no.
Winding our way from our head to our toes.
And this is how it goes.

Ya see, baby I woke up this morning smiling.
Remembering the night before I'm reeling.
Fingers down my body, was I dreaming?
Feeling our sexy, was I treating you right?
Baby I could go all night.
Got me coming back for more.
Like I wanna be your toy.

When I woke up this morning, I was smiling!
Throwing off my PJs, was I dreaming?
Feeling hot under the collar we were reeling and
steaming.
Tell me baby, am I dreaming? Yeah, we started
off slow and then we steamed in.

Discovering our passion, it was rising.
You work my body good, there's no denying it boy.
Licking and stroking 'til we both shiver with joy.
You took your time with me baby, now I'm reeled in.
And all I can think of, is how you're feelin?
Just wanna please ya.
And next time I come over, gonna show ya.

Now kiss me long and hard, so I remember.
How you touched me baby, was oh so tender.
Skin on skin, eyes to eyes, with such a sweetness.
That gentle loving touch is now my weakness.
Can I have a witness, to share this, one more kiss.
Come and put it on me.

Watch me smiling and see.

And now I'm smiling!
I hope you're smiling.
I woke up smiling...

23 April 2018

35 FERVENT KISSES

Fervent kisses, fleeting glances.
Looking for love but scared of chancing.
Hurt by lessons slapped and taught. Lingered
looks which search through fraught.
Gentle steps, the chance we took.
Sharing secrets, tenterhooks.
Hope is veiled in pain with kiss.
Learning where to find our bliss.
Questions, histories, memories, sharing.
Tender, tearful moments, caring.
No desire for past behaviour.
Will it be fleeting or is this the major?
Smiles of kindness but scared of hurting.
Vintage heartache, old love scars.
Romance required, the moon and stars.
New love style too quick, too easy.
Old romantics, young and breezy.
Tread slowly now, where fools rush in.
Slowly learning, drink it in.
Stolen moments, taking chances.
Romantic music, close, slow dances.
Shall we take a chance and risk.
Love flickers through that sweet first kiss.

14 February 2019

36 THE WORDSMITH

Words are MY medium.
So TELL me how you're feeling.
Talk to me with whispers.
Let no miscommunication fester.
Reach out with honesty and speak to me with clarity.
Let the lyrical illiteracy of spoken word or poetry.
Drip with soft alacrity and trickle down to chat with me.
Words are MY medium.
Let no objective nouns rip into me.
Explain your adverbs carefully.
Punctuate where necessary.
And let's see where this takes us, literally.
Sound the words out specifically.
And hear the magic speak to me
A sentence worth repeating to me.
Is that you are in love with me.
Those three little words in the dictionary
Are the most important, romantically.
Like a romance novel, use your ink and quill.
Scribe your feelings on the page, just spill.
So use your words and speak to me.
Like an artist, create a canvas for me.

Fill it with positivity and energy.
Feel your words caress, as they envelope me.
Hear the diction sing to me.
Pronunciation, clear to me.
Then softly say "au revoir" to me.
In any language you fancy, "Si?".
You see words are MY medium.
And that's how you'll stand out to me.
So, enunciate with precision please.
And you can leave the rest to me.

25 April 2018

37 YOU WANT TO DOMINATE ME?

So, you want to rule me?
Lead, govern and direct me?
Spank me, beat me, hit, then take me?
But then you want to kiss and bait me?

Go gentle with your hands please, Sir.
If I'm your pussycat, make me purr.
But watch out for the Minx inside.
I'll scratch and bite, don't be surprised.

Bite my neck watch Vampira rise.
Look deeper into my turquoise eyes.
Nipples harden, arching back.
Your hand delivers ringing slap.

A wicked smile is fleeting here.
The sting of pain may draw a tear.
Then kiss me, tender, rivers run.
Tease me with your liquid tongue.

Feel the ebb and watch my flow.
Flip me over, here we go...
Master this and master me.
Master, F*&k me, masterfully.

Mistress Angelica
18 July 2014

38 MISTRESS ANGELICA

Darkness falls and creatures surface.
Dungeon Masters; here comes The Mistress.
Light the candles, melting wax.
Polish every whip to crack.

Ready the silken ropes for bondage.
In this place She feeds your damage.
Chains are shackled, padlocks ready.
She's in charge now; best hold steady.

Watch the flickering waxy melts
Incoming; Fire and fury welts.
Beg for soothing ice relief.
Switch or Sub? Grit your teeth!

Feel the air of dripping fear.
Your heart doth quicken when She's near.
Her pleasure as she warms your cheek.
Her Parlour, where your pain is reaped.

Erotic role play, this; Her Stage.
You WILL immerse and fully engage.
The journey begins, She'll lead the way.
To reach your brink again, AGAIN.

Commanding every breath you take.
She'll rattle you, make no mistake.
She'll decide if you've been good.
Caress your paralysed and straining wood.

Or slap your face and bite your neck.
You'll never know what's coming next.
Obey and push on, don't be weak.
Eyes down you try to glance and peep.

This stunning beauty, cold as ice.
Will warm you up, before she strikes.
If Mistress pleases, you'll be in luck.
Or you'll lick her boots clean of muck.

Formidable, shining rubber Goddess.
Will test your limits, at your duress.
Menacing and deftly agile.
Please Her and She may just smile.

But don't be disrespectful Slave.
Or the punishment will be grave.
One hard crack of Her riding crop.
Enough to limp the hardest cock.

Tied in leather strapped and full.
On your knees, tied tight and pull.
"Wriggle at your peril, Rat."
Mistress's disapproving spat.

Saliva on your face; a lesson.
Your pain will escalate, not lessen.
She'll eb and flow you, peak and trough.
"You're worthless, MINE, I own you, Sloth."

Please Her and Mistress may grace with touch.
Or just electrocute your withered crutch.
Blindfold on and cuffs extended.
Beg for mercy on knees, a bended.

Shackled to Spread bar - legs apart.
Prepare yourself, it's time to start.
Senses heightened, feel Her presence
This dangerous game belies her essence.

You shiver; adrenaline is surging.
Shame-ridden as you lay there purging.
Goosebumps on anticipating neck.
You are Hers; you're at her beck.

Stroking, slapping, teasing biting.
This trip of Darkness is so inviting.
Round and round you're in a spin.
Playing to her every whim.

Excitement rises, what's the play?
The best part of your wicked day.
Will She suffocate or gag and chain?
At Her pleasure, will be your pain.

As you cower, bend and straddle.
She might slap you, with Her studded paddle.
"Bend over!" She's accurate and strict.
You won't even feel it, She's so quick.

Wait for the exquisite sting.
No relenting or safe word screaming.
Sliding on the edge of danger.
She ties her prey; a waiting stranger.

There are no constraints here, only yours.
Open up your Subby doors.
This is the nightly dance of terror.
To underestimate Her, will be your error.

In this room, your pain is Her pleasure.
She'll unlock your BDSM treasure.
Eyes down, and don't you dare address Her.
Here She comes,
Yes, Mistress Angelica.

Mistress Angelica
12 February 2021

39 THE MASTER

You rule me rigid, as I serve.
Bowed and cowering, I will learn.
Deprive my lust and lead away.
My spirit broken, I'm your slave.

Tend me softly, wringing slap.
Bind me gently, ankles wrapped.
Welts of hate adorn my torso.
Bleeding cuts and scars of old.

So, punish me for past behaviour.
Rescue me, my evil saviour.
Basking in your mind so clever.
No-one reached me like this, ever.

Yearning for your mind to slay me.
Twist and turn me, don't forsake me.
Master, I beg for your forgiveness.
Cease my bitter, impatient weakness.

Hold me in your high esteem.
Kiss me, lick me, teach me, please.
Feed me daily with your lesson.
Every day my pride will lessen.

Slave positions - Master teach me.
Lead me to the darkness in me.
Humbled Master, I'm on my knees.
Head bowed, tongue out, I beg you please.

Own me Master, I'll be yours.
Always at your service doors.
Begging for my Master's voice.
I'm your servant, there's no choice.

Master, I am all for you.
Anything, I'd do for you.
Bind me Master, rule me King.
Kiss me, thrill me - make me sing.

I promise to be good, Sir please.
Head bowed, hands tied, on my knees.
You are the architect I need.
You've built desire inside of me.

Master make me yours, I beg you.
Your Slave, your Doll, I will forever serve you.

01 April 2021

40 JUST ONE OF
THOSE FRIENDS

These days, you only call me at the weekend.
Now a days, I only see you when you need me.
Less and less unless you're going on a bender.
Head down, note rolled; ready for the dopamine
blender.

Hear the packet rustle from a mile away.
Phone's off, but you're knocking at my door
anyway.
Ring the doorbell like Jehovah.
Witness your demise, with a bone like Rover.

But you're just one of those friends, that I won't
miss.
Just one of those friends who takes the piss.

These are the Champagne and the Charlie days.
Late nights, first class, private jets, and fast
lanes.
Calf leather interior and caviar on an ice platter
Blood diamonds dripping like a snowball splatter.

Packet's getting smaller; a dilemma.
Missing digits in a fury, hand tremors.
On the phone again you dial the number.
Are you a VIP or just a basic member?

In a lightbulb moment, we were "best mates".
You decided in a heartbeat, said I was "great".
Listen to this bullshit that I'm hearing.
Hear what, don't take the piss, I'm not your China.
You're greedy and you're buzzed; that's not my drama.

But you're just one of those friends, that I won't miss.
Just one of those friends who takes the piss.

These are the Champagne and the Charlie days.
Late nights, first class, private jets, and fast lanes.
Calf leather interior and caviar on an ice platter
Blood diamonds dripping like a snowball splatter.

You're just a user, paying over with your paper.
Guess what, I listen to your bullshit and I play ya.
Take the money from your hand, you give it quick time.
Thanks though, cos I've got a nice crib and a flash ride.
Then I see you on the street and you just walk by.
With your girl who doesn't know, it's what you're hiding.
Silent nod, head down, you give me side eye.

But you're just one of those friends, that I won't miss.
Just one of those friends who takes the piss.

These are the Champagne and the Charlie days.
Late nights, first class, private jets, and fast lanes.
Calf leather interior and caviar on an ice platter
Blood diamonds dripping like a snowball splatter.

Call the chauffeur, get a pick-up, bring your girlfriend.
Park the F12 and the Aston, bring the Black Benz.
Going all day and all night it is relentless.
This super yao powder makes you fearless.

But you're just one of those friends, that I won't miss.
Just one of those friends who takes the piss.

These days, you only call me at the weekend.
Now a days, I only see you when you need me.
Less and less unless you're going on a bender.
Head down, note rolled; ready for the dopamine blender.

You ring my phone and I don't answer.
I'm busy bud... I got my own thing.
Can't keep dropping what I'm doing to deliver your ching!

Switch my phone off, count the money, now I'm out.
Thanks for the business, but I'm out.
No more pills, ketamine, mandy or snout.

Wrapping up the business – it's a good day.
Hanging up the burner had my pay day.
Thank you but it's time to go.
Ring ring. Ring ring.
Hello?....

12 April 2021

41 THE SEASONS

"I'll be back", the Sun whispered, as the skies filled up with rain.

Fear not, as everything that goes around, comes around again.

As Jack Frost gently blows his icy breath into the breeze.

Summer nights begin to fade, replaced with boots in rustling leaves.

It's ok, because we have warmth inside, with marshmallows floating there.

We're thankful for heating, cosy fires and fluffy socks for you to wear.

"Don't worry" sing the Trees, as they shed their red and golden leaves. "We nourish the earth to feed our roots, it's not as bad as it may seem."

"Our leaves will grow again next Spring, the Sun will come, you'll see."

So meanwhile let's build snowmen and make amazing memories.

Next you'll know, Santa's on his way; across the world he flies.

Then New Year fireworks celebrations light-up every sky.

The Seasons come and go each year – the seeds of change will flow.

That every Season has its job, is reassuring for us to know.

The trick is to embrace each Season, for all that it will bring.

Everything for a reason and soon Summer days again will sing.

14 September 2021

42 HURRICANE LIFE

I saw a post on Linked In #thislittlegirlisme.

Followed by an explanation of women's challenges and successes; and this caption:

"I'm sharing this with you because 70% of girls feel more confident about their futures after hearing from women role models, supporting them with statements like "it's ok to fail, it's ok to make mistakes" and "it's ok not to be ok".

So, # This little girl is ME...

As I stared at the photo of the little girl I used to be.
Full of promise, hope; innocent, playful and pretty.
I re-wound my life in my head, like an old VHS tape.
And as it paused and flickered before me.
I tried to extricate the events which had shaped me.
To facilitate the point of the post I was writing.

As I started to write my own version.
I tried to snapshot the things I had overcome.
And as I bullet-pointed my life into a perfectly written, listed presentation, I paused for a while. I don't know many girls on Linked-in who would feel more confident after reading anyone's whirlwind of a life, let alone mine.

I'm not sure I could write a post short enough to get the message across and then calmly state at the end that "it's ok, not to be ok".

Because it wasn't.
It wasn't okay.
I was never "okay".

My life was a fucking Hurricane.
An "act of God" which just kept on coming.

A fight from the start - adopted at birth, disliked and envied by my adopted mother.
It was lonely.

A dark and hidden riptide.
Pulling me down, swirling me side to side, when no-one was looking.
Ducking me under the water and immersing me in the pain of the sting as the salt water bathed my never-ending wounds.

I grew up in a world of shame and disappointment.
A smile from a stranger would be my Savlon; my ointment.
And for a while, until he died, my Dad was my saviour.

Life, was a freaking Tornedo.
Gale-force trauma at its best.
I was thrown from one world of pain to the next like a rag doll.
No rest for the wicked.
Death, rejection, rape and beatings.
Disaster, upon disaster.
It just kept on coming.
The darkness came and the lightning struck.
The storms just didn't subside.

No social media post could condense it.
It was savage and relentless.

How I survived thus far is either a miracle or just because it's not done yet and there's even more torment ahead.

Stand strong, clenched fists and gritted teeth.
Adrenaline kicks in with cortisol release.
Fight or flight?
Dig-in, steadfast, hold tight.

Oh, don't worry - I'll fight.

Even now, with the tirade of traumatic interludes which can't be jotted down on a snippy post to encourage other women to have faith and stay strong by seeing the pain we've all been through to get "here" on Linked in; apparently "doing better".
Or wining or succeeding – despite everything.

Pat on the back - does that help you my Sisters?
Stiff upper lip?
More like fat lip and blisters.
From the frost-bitten cold front, bluster of the easterly winds of winter.
I've been whip-lashed by the down-pour.
And I'm reeling from the icy splinters.

How can my Hurricane be subjugated into a neat little box and laid to rest as if the seas are now calm just to encourage a girl I never met to be a better person when she hasn't even weathered her own storm in a teacup yet?

My survival is a constant battle.
Not a Ted Talk waiting to happen and a round of applause because I weathered MY storm and here – look at me now!
As I walk off stage straight into the next puddle.

Here we go again.
It's starting to rain.
Brolly at the ready, zip up, batten down the hatches, off we go again.

Welcome to Hurricane "Life".

You're in the eye of the storm.
But now it's almost normal to be here.
The comforting ecstasy of the familiar pain.

I love the way they always give it a woman's name.

Hurricane Rita?
Rita sounds like a pussy cat to be honest.

How about Hurricane "Bitch of a mother"?

Or Hurricane "I was abused by my brother"?

Don't forget Hurricane "Rapist", or Hurricane "Beat you 'til you're barely breathing"?

And Hurricane "Sorry you couldn't have kids, but I'd rather sniff coke, so I'm leaving"?

Or Hurricane "How many times can I break your heart and leave you reeling"?

Sorry to say, but there's plenty more where that came from.

Like Hurricane "Miscarriage", and Hurricane "Death of your Father"? or Hurricane "Divorce" and Hurricane "Date Rape".

I could go on.

But that's not the object of this hashtag, is it? We are supposed to be positive and inspiring. Not bitter and whining.

Sure, I'm a work in progress. I confess. I'll take it all on the chin, with no regrets.

Platitudes won't make a difference. Do they ever?

Not to someone who's indifferent to the weather.

Everyone has a storm to ride, but whether they survive and thrive is the question.

And so, it's HOW you get through it.
Now THAT's the lesson.

So, apologies if I've shocked you.
The object was not to make things awkward.
I just gave you a jab from my lightning rod.
To see if you've got the stomach for the journey.
To test the waters and see if you're storm-worthy.
So please don't judge for me for my honesty, and burn me.
Or make assumptions, turn away from me or spurn me.

Oh, don't get me wrong, I'm not done yet.

Because whatever it brought thus far, didn't manage to kill me.
I'll make that decision when I'm ready.

I'll stand in my Hurricane until I'm done.
There'll be no shelter from My Cyclone, these are MY terms.

You can't ravage the ravaged and win.
Trust me.
I've been the student, now I'm YOUR adversary.
See my previous form, and please don't underestimate me.

Hurricane "Life" will be MY victory.
Just in case you were in any doubt.

Don't be.

3 September 2021

43 SUICIDAL MANIAC

I'm the gobby nutter.
You'll hear me down the street.
I'm the one who laughs so loud,
My eyebrows nearly meet.

I'm the sobbing wreck.
The one who's wailing in her grief.
I'm the caring neighbour who'll always
acknowledge you on our street.

I'm the one who'll show up.
On the day you need a friend.
I'm the one who'll hold your hair.
I'm the fixer; "Captain Mend".

I'm the emotional Bionic Woman.
Who's been mended way too many times.
I'm the broken-hearted girl.
Who's dying day by day, inside.

I'm the childless mother.
The loss of nurture's silent killer.
I'm the IVF rejection letter.
With smothering pillow and extra filler.

I'm the menopausal rollercoaster.
The ride that won't subside. The white-knuckle,
life-threatening, one-of life's best moments.
I'm your ride or die.

I'm the melancholy moments.
I'm the tissue box re-refill.
I'm the drop the mic; the final curtain.
I'm the storm. then I'm the still.

I'm the fighter, I'm the steadfast.
I'm the "rom-com's" shining hero.
I'll give it everything I've got.
But now, all I've got to give, is Zero.

I'm the stranger full of mystery.
I'm the friendly, local girl.
I'm the road-rage, middle finger.
I'm the wind within the whirl.

I'm the tourist in a strange place.
No Lonely Planet guide for me.
I don't know what the future holds.
Some days it's only darkness that I see.

I'm the author of this ditty.
I'm the girl who rhymes her words.
So, if you're reading this and I'm no more.
Please read them all and learn.

I'm the "Our Tune" on the radio.
I'll let you know when I am sad.
If I call and say "I need you".
Just come, and sit, and hold my hand.

I'm your thirty second countdown.
Your conundrum to unscramble.
The goodbye letters written
May not be eloquent, and may ramble.

I'm the one you will remember.
Whose heart adorned her tattooed sleeve.
I'm the arms in the air House Diva.
But now it's time to leave.

Head held high, high heels in hand.
Barefoot I will go.
Back to dust and memories.
Where no more pain can grow.

I'm the suicidal maniac.
I gave it my best shot.
I'm just a sad girl, who's suicidal.
So, stop the world, I'm getting off.

7 November 2021

THE END

That's it... I really hope you enjoyed.

I'm sorry if some of those were a bit hard-hitting.

It's important to know, that I write to process my emotions and it really helps me when I'm in love, or happy but especially, when I'm sad.

Here's some helpful numbers should you feel like talking.

SAMARITANS UK Call 116 123 Free

Whatever you're going through, a Samaritan will face it with you. They're there 24 hours a day, 365 days a year.

They do not judge, they won't lecture you, they just listen and understand.

Sometimes, that's all you need.

CALM Call 0800 58 58 58 Free

People experience suicidal thoughts for many reasons – and they can be a result of a combination of things and there is nothing wrong with you if you, or the person you care about, is experiencing thoughts about taking their own life.

If you or someone you know is experiencing suicidal thoughts, it is important to tell someone about them and get some help. You can contact the CALM helpline between 5pm-midnight or call 999 if you or someone you know is in immediate danger.

No matter how you're feeling, or what situation you're in, there's always a way forward – even if it doesn't feel that way right now.

Remember, it's good to talk,
or just write it down.
Be safe out there.